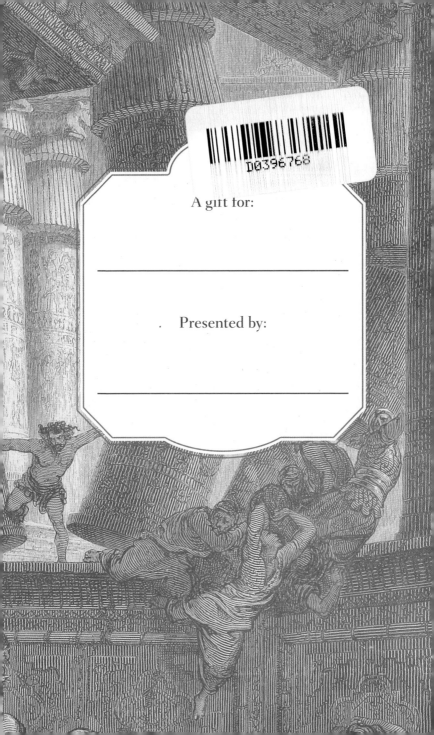

A gift for:

_____

Presented by:

_____

Contents

CONTENTS

CONTENTS

CONTENTS

Introduction

It's no exaggeration to say that allusions from Bible stories still remain part of our everyday lives. When you accuse someone of babbling on and on, or describe your friend as a Good Samaritan, you may not realize you are referring back to the biblical stories of the Tower of Babel and Jesus's parable of the Good Samaritan. The Bible has been the world's best-selling book for hundreds of years—and no book can match its sales figures, even today. In fact, Bible sales make the sales of the Harry Potter and Hunger Games series and every other book pale in comparison.

When we dig below the surface of our cultural fads and preferences, we find the Bible in a surprising number of places. For example, if you've ever told someone not to take "an eye for an eye," that's from the Bible.[1] If you've ever accomplished something "by the skin of your teeth"[2] or been told you're the "apple of" someone's eye,[3] those phrases are from the Bible, too.

On the other hand, some people view the Bible,

especially in its older editions and translations, as a piece of antiquated history. It's a huge tome, for one thing—more than two thousand pages in most versions—and people have trouble with those thin, flimsy pages and the archaic, tiny print. The Bible also describes ancient, unfamiliar traditions and customs, and the people who quote from it often sound like they're reading Shakespeare when they say "thou" and "thine" and all that. They don't realize there are many user-friendly versions of the Bible, with scores of notes and modern analyses in which these timeless narratives come alive. This is what we have attempted to do in this volume—make some of the major stories accessible, enjoyable, and inspiring.

The Bible is a major influence on the moral and social codes that teach us what's right and wrong, acceptable and unacceptable. It's where our society learned the Golden Rule, for example—that we should treat others as we'd like to be treated.[4] In addition, Jesus taught us to love our enemies as well as our neighbors,[5] and the Bible's Ten Commandments[6] are the foundation of the Western judicial system.

Even our primary forms of entertainment have at times been (and continue to be) heavily influenced by the Bible. Most examples of great literature—from Shakespeare's works to Dickens to Cormac McCarthy—contain several allusions to scriptural texts and events, as do the works of several great songwriters, including Bob Dylan, Johnny Cash, Sting, and many more. Even movies and television have mined the Scriptures for decades. Just a couple of examples: you can't really understand some of the themes in *The Matrix* without a basic knowledge of the Bible; and biblical themes are implicit in *The Lord of the Rings*.

When you get down to it, we shouldn't be surprised by the Bible's entrenchment in modern society. Stories have always had the power to move us, motivate us, unsettle us, and inspire us to become the people we've been created to be. And at its core, the Bible is a collection of some of the best-loved and most influential stories ever told.

You'll find a lot of those stories summarized in the following pages. As you read, keep in mind the different ways these stories have influenced not only the outside world but your own life as well. Perhaps your mother first read them to you as you sat comfortably in her lap; perhaps you heard them in Sunday school, or when you took a course in classic literature. Most important, whether you're experiencing them again or encountering them for the first time, allow yourself to be enriched as you dig into Bible stories you may have forgotten.

PART I
The Old Testament

One Bad Apple
Spoils the World

Adam and Eve
(Genesis 2:15–3:24)

When you hear the word "paradise," what images come to mind? Maybe you think of a deserted island—sandy beaches surrounded by clear, crystal-blue water. Or maybe you picture mountains covered with the kind of powdery snow that's perfect for skiing. Maybe it's a bustling city street packed with gourmet restaurants and Starbucks coffeehouses on every corner.

Whatever your particular vision of paradise may be, try to hold it in your mind as we explore the story of Adam and Eve—the first human beings to live, love, cry, and die on planet Earth.

A Single Guy

According to Genesis 1 (the first chapter of the first book in the Bible), God created the entire universe in just six days. He started with raw materials such as light, water, air, and land. Then He created specific objects to make use of those raw materials. He created the sun, moon, and stars to produce and reflect light. He created fish for the water, birds for the air, and plants and animals for the land.

Then, on the sixth day, God created His crowning achievement: human beings. Technically, though, He started by creating a single human being. That was Adam, the world's first man.

If you're hoping Adam lived in the world's first man cave, I'm afraid you're out of luck. God actually planted a garden paradise in a land called Eden, and that became Adam's home. According to Genesis 2, the Garden of Eden was filled with "trees that were pleasing to the eye and good for food."[7]

Adam wasn't a layabout; even in the middle of paradise, he was given a job. Specifically, God made Adam a steward of His creation. That didn't mean Adam was the owner of the garden or any other part of the created world, nor could he use and abuse creation to satisfy his whims. Rather, Adam was charged with the task of tending and caring for both the garden he lived in and the other creatures that lived with him. Adam even had the privilege of naming the different species of plants and animals as he saw fit.

For a time, everything was perfect. Adam was strong, smart, and confident. He found satisfaction in his work, pleasure in his connections with the other living things around him, and joy in his relationship with God, who had created him. It was a heavenly experience.

A Perfect Match

After a time, however, it became clear that Adam was unique among all the animals in creation. Whereas male birds could connect with female birds, and each squirrel scampering through the trees could find community and companionship among the other squirrels, Adam was alone. He was quite literally "one of a kind."

In time, God remedied this situation by creating Eve—the world's first woman. It's interesting that God didn't create Eve from scratch, as He'd done with Adam. Instead, He performed the world's first surgical procedure by placing Adam in a deep sleep (the world's first anesthesia, apparently), removing one of Adam's ribs, and using that bone as the raw material with which to create Eve.

Suddenly, shockingly, Adam was no longer unique. And that was a good thing because wonderfully, happily, he was no longer alone.

Adam and Eve were the perfect embodiment of what a man and a woman can be. They were physically unblemished, mentally secure, and emotionally unscarred—think of the movie *Gattaca* without the eugenics and genetic deception. It gets better, though. Not only were Adam and Eve the personifications of perfection as human beings, but they were perfectly made for each other. They enjoyed a faultless, flawless relationship as husband and wife. Best of all, they enjoyed a faultless, flawless relationship with God.

Basically, Adam and Eve were each in heaven, and each had the privilege of sharing heaven with the other.

For a time . . .

Damaged Goods

They say good things never last, and, sadly, that was the case for the perfect life Adam and Eve shared in the Garden of Eden. Everything unraveled in an instant because of a single, catastrophic choice. Before we get to that choice, however, we need a little backstory.

When God created the Garden of Eden, He planted two trees in its center: "the tree of life and the tree of the knowledge of good and evil."[8] Adam and Eve were encouraged to enjoy every aspect of their garden home—except that second tree. The tree of the knowledge of good and evil was off-limits, and God warned His creations that they would "certainly die" if they consumed its fruit.

In case you're wondering, this setup wasn't some malevolent game God wanted to play. Rather, the forbidden tree was a physical manifestation of Adam and Eve's free will—their ability to choose between right and wrong.

What happened next was tragic. Adam and Eve were in the garden together when Eve was approached by a serpent. Strangely enough, this serpent could talk. Stranger still, it spoke falsely to Eve. It told her she wouldn't die if she ate the fruit from the forbidden tree; quite the opposite. The snake promised she would gain new understanding and become like God.

You know how the story goes from there. Tempted by the sweetness of the fruit and beguiled by the chance to become equal with God, Eve took the bait and took a bite. Then she gave some fruit to Adam, and he followed suit. They both made a terrible mistake by rejecting God in favor of pleasure and personal gain.

And it cost them. Big-time. They became aware of good and evil because they allowed the seeds of evil to germinate in their hearts—and those seeds have been producing new and terrible fruit within and among the human race ever since. Adam and Eve became broken and flawed, and the world broke along with them. That's why their epic mistake is usually referred to as "the fall."

God didn't want Adam and Eve to live forever in their damaged state, so He sent them away from the Garden of Eden, away from the tree of life. They lived out the rest of their days the same way we all do. They had good times and bad times. They loved and laughed and fought and grew old—and eventually the first man and woman created to enjoy the earth passed out of the world and into someplace new.

Key Bible Passage to Remember

"And I will put enmity between you and the woman, and between your offspring and hers; he will crush your head, and you will strike his heel." (Genesis 3:15)

God is speaking to the serpent (Satan), telling him that down through the ages his evil forces will oppose the human race and vice versa. Christians believe this is the first prophecy to mention a Messiah, who will die (strike his heel) but ultimately crush the evil forces who oppose the human race.

A Boatload of Trouble

Noah and the Ark
(Genesis 6:11–9:17)

When the weather turns hot, you know it's summer blockbuster season. And nothing says popcorn like a movie about the end of the world, right?

Through the magic of special effects, films such as *The Day After Tomorrow* and *2012* have given us a glimpse of what it might actually look like if the planet were ravaged by a series of cataclysmic natural disasters—earthquakes, tornadoes, huge tidal waves—and if celebrities flew from city to city attempting to rescue their families.

But when Hollywood producers gear up for their next IMAX spectacular, they won't need screenwriters to come up with some off-the-wall plot. All they need to do is adapt one of the oldest stories ever written: Noah and the ark. This worldwide flood would make the weather in *The Perfect Storm* look like a gentle spring drizzle!

A Huge Building Project

In the same way that Adam was unique in the Garden of Eden before the creation of Eve, Noah was also unique among the people of his day. In spite of the evil around him, "Noah was a righteous man, blameless among the people of his time, and he walked faithfully with God."[9]

Because of Noah's faithfulness, he received the ultimate piece of insider information: God planned to slow down the massive flood of evil in the world by wiping out the human population and starting over—with Noah as the new Adam. Talk about pressure!

God gave Noah detailed instructions for two major projects. First, He commanded Noah to build a large boat, also called an ark, and load it with supplies for him and his family. Second, God told Noah to build the ark so that it could hold a lot of animals: "Two of every kind of bird, of every kind of animal and of every kind of creature that moves along the ground will come to you to be kept alive."[10] More pressure!

Now, the ark had to be absolutely massive to accommodate so many creatures. It needed to be more than 450 feet long, 75 feet wide, and 45 feet high—which means it would barely fit into most NFL stadiums. A daunting task, to say the least, but Noah and his sons worked hard, and they eventually got the job done. When construction was complete, God told Noah to take his family onto the ark and batten down the hatches. They weren't the only ones finding their staterooms, of course. The text says, "Pairs of all creatures that have the breath of life in them came to Noah and entered the ark."[11]

When everyone and everything was loaded up, God sealed the door of the ark. And then things started to get rough. Rain began to pour from the sky. The "springs of the great deep burst forth."[12] The flood had begun.

Water, Water Everywhere

The Bible says rain fell on the earth for forty days and forty nights, and the floodwaters rose throughout the land until even the mountains were covered. The end of Genesis 7 includes this haunting sentence: "Only Noah was left, and those with him in the ark."[13]

The Scriptures don't provide any details about what Noah and his family experienced during the flood, but it's safe to say they were longing for some new board games by the time the boat struck land on Mount Ararat. They'd been at sea for five months by then, and it was more than two months later when Noah and his family were finally able to see the tops of the mountains around them as the water continued to recede.

For another three months, Noah and his family tried to figure out when it would be safe to disembark.

They sent out birds to do a little scouting for them, and when a dove came back with an olive leaf in its beak, they knew things were headed in the right direction.

A Promise of Never Again

Finally, more than a year after the flood began, Noah and his family left the ark with the animals. One of the first things Noah did after settling down on dry land was build an altar and make sacrifices to God in order to show how thankful he was that he and his family had been spared. (He was a righteous guy, remember?)

When God saw the offerings, He made a covenant with Noah—a legally binding promise. Never again would He curse the planet because of human evil, and never again would He send a flood to destroy all the people of the earth. God even used rainbows as a visible confirmation of that promise.

God also gave a new command to Noah and his family: "As for you, be fruitful and increase in number; multiply on the earth and increase upon it."[14] This is the same command God had given to Adam and Eve, and it confirmed that He was once again forging a relationship with His people on earth.

Key Bible Passage to Remember

"And God said, 'This is the sign of the covenant I am making between me and you and every living creature with you, a covenant for all generations to come . . .'" (Genesis 9:12)

God's covenant extends to "all generations" of human beings, which includes those of us alive today. It also paves the way for God's covenant with Abraham and his descendants, the Jews—plus the new covenant offered by Jesus to any who choose to follow Him.

The Skyscraper
That Didn't Scrape

The Tower of Babel
(Genesis 11:1–9)

When you think of the most famous buildings in the world, how many of them are skyscrapers? Sure, something like the Louvre in Paris is pretty neat, and you can't get much fancier than the Taj Mahal. But think of the Empire State Building in New York, or the Willis Tower in Chicago (formerly the Sears Tower). Think of Tom Cruise running down the side of the Burj Khalifa in *Mission: Impossible—Ghost Protocol*.

In truth, few things epitomize the human spirit better than a really, *really* tall building.

Unfortunately, the men and women behind the world's first attempted skyscraper epitomized the darker elements of that spirit—idolatry, pride, and a hunger for power. The end result was the confusing mess we know today as the Tower of Babel.

High Tech Growing Higher

Although nobody knows the exact dates, the events surrounding the construction and collapse of the Tower of Babel took place several generations after Noah and his family used the ark to ride out a worldwide flood. The Bible identifies the setting of the story as "a plain in Shinar."[15] That particular part of the world would later be known as Babylon, and today we know it as Iraq.

The plot of the story is fairly simple. A large group of people decided to journey eastward, away from the civilizations that had been established by Noah's descendants. These people were trailblazers who chose to explore new areas of the world—"to boldly go where no man has gone before," if you're a *Star Trek* fan.

As they traveled, they stumbled upon an ideal parcel of land. It was a level plain, and because we know that ancient Babylon was located near the intersection of the Tigris and Euphrates Rivers, it would have been a fertile plain, with water nearby. Apparently this particular stretch of land was so perfect that the travelers couldn't pass it up. They abandoned their exploratory journey and decided to settle down.

More than that, they decided to build a city. These people had made some technological advancements, and they were able to use oven-baked bricks in their construction—which were much sturdier and more scalable than the rough-hewn rocks used in other parts of the ancient world at that time.

Because of these bricks, the people decided to add something completely new to their city: "Then they said, 'Come, let us build ourselves a city, with a tower that reaches to the heavens, so that we may make a name for ourselves; otherwise we will be scattered over the face of the whole earth.'"[16]

And that's when they got themselves in some serious trouble.

Heavens Above!

In order to wrap our minds around the main conflict in this story—and its resolution—we need to answer two questions that invariably pop up regarding this portion of the plot. Here's the first: *How did the people expect to reach the heavens with a building?* They didn't think they could build something high enough to touch the sky, right?

Well, actually, that's exactly what the tower builders planned to do. In the ancient world, people didn't have any comprehension of the atmosphere and its layers of gases and all that. Rather, they thought the sky was a solid object—a huge sheet of rock that covered the earth. They believed the sun, moon, and stars were carved into or hung from the sky, and that those heavenly bodies traveled through the sky when the huge sheet of rock rotated above them.

So the builders' goal was to build a tower that literally scraped the sky. Then they planned to carve a hole in the sheet of rock, climb through, and announce, "We're here!" to the inhabitants of heaven.

Here's the second question: *What's the big deal?* Why did God care if the people wanted to settle down and build a big tower—especially if He knew they would never actually be able to achieve their goal of reaching His dwelling place?

There are a couple of reasons why their attempt at a tower mattered. First, remember that God had commanded Noah and his descendants to "Be fruitful and increase in number and fill the earth."[17] Well, by deciding to settle down in one place and build a great city, the Babylonians were disobeying God's command to "fill the earth." They were ducking out of their part in God's plan to establish humanity throughout the world.

Second, by establishing a connection between earth and heaven, the tower builders hoped to "make a name" for themselves by reaching God's dwelling place. Bursting with pride, they wanted to be on the same level with God—which was the same reason Adam and Eve ate the forbidden fruit; they wanted to "be like God."[18]

All Fall Down

God was aware of the tower builders' activity, of course—and their underlying motivations. He understood that people could get themselves into a lot of trouble by working together to accomplish such a sinful goal, so He took action.

The text emphasizes twice that God decided to "go down" to the earth and deal with the tower builders' rebellion. There's some intentional humor in that emphasis. It's as if God was making light of their plans to reach Him with their tower. He was saying, "Well, if they haven't gotten up here yet, I may as well go down there and see what all the fuss is about."

God's solution to the whole affair was to confuse the languages of the tower builders. One night everyone went to bed speaking the same language, but when they woke up the next morning, different groups of people spoke completely different languages. The text says, "That is why it was called Babel," which is a funny play on words—the Hebrew word for "babble" (one might also say "gibberish" or "gobbledygook") sounds similar to the word for Babylon.

In the end, the tower builders were forced to abandon their project because of communication issues. Unable to understand one other, the people scattered and settled in different places across the face of the earth—as God intended.

Key Bible Passage to Remember

"Then they said, 'Come, let us build ourselves a city, with a tower that reaches to the heavens . . .'"(Genesis 11:4)

People have always had a desire to connect with God in some way. The tower builders' attempt was foolish, but it foreshadows God's efforts to maintain a relationship with us through the Patriarchs, the Prophets, and ultimately through Jesus Christ.

His Birthright
for a Bowl of Stew

There have been a number of seriously deceptive scam artists in human history—both real and imagined. Frank Abagnale is one of the more famous con men from modern times. Portrayed by Leonardo DiCaprio in the movie *Catch Me If You Can*, Abagnale spent decades passing bad checks and masquerading as various authority figures before he was finally captured in New York City.

They didn't have bank checks or deposit slips in the ancient world, of course. But that didn't stop one of the Bible's major characters from getting scammed out of house and home.

The Abraham Before Lincoln

For the Jewish people, no historical figures are more famous or revered than the Patriarchs: Abraham,

Isaac, and Jacob. In fact, the way Jews feel about the Patriarchs is similar to the way many Americans feel about the Founding Fathers, including George Washington, Thomas Jefferson, and Benjamin Franklin— except the Patriarchs precede the Founding Fathers by many thousands of years.

Abraham, the first and most famous of the Patriarchs, was the great-great-great-great-great-great-great-grandson of Noah. Abraham married Sarah, who, at the age of ninety, miraculously gave birth to Isaac. Isaac married a woman named Rebekah, who became pregnant with twin boys named Jacob and Esau.

Trouble Brewing

At first, Rebekah wasn't aware she was carrying twins. She only knew there was some serious kicking happening inside her belly, and it became so violent she cried out to God in order to ask what was happening to her.

God's answer was shocking in a number of ways, "Two nations are in your womb," He said, "and two peoples from within you will be separated; one people will be stronger than the other, and the older will serve the younger."[21] Jacob and Esau were struggling against each other even in the womb. More important, God proclaimed that the older son would serve the younger—an extraordinary statement in a culture that almost always favored the oldest son.

Unfortunately, things didn't calm down for the brothers after they were born. The text says, "Esau became a skillful hunter, a man of the open country," while Jacob "was content to stay at home among the tents."[22] In other words, if their story were to become a Hollywood movie, the role of Esau would go to someone like Gerard Butler or Russell Crowe. Jacob would probably be played by Elijah Wood.

One day, Esau was absolutely famished when he came home from hunting in the wilderness. He'd worked up quite an appetite doing manly things, and he noticed right away that his brother was cooking up a big batch of spicy, savory stew. He said, "Quick, let me have some of that red stew!"[23]

Jacob saw a chance to advance his own position, so he answered by saying, "First sell me your birth-right."[24] Now, this was an outrageous demand. It would be as if you walked into a McDonald's, ordered a Big Mac with fries and a Coke, and then heard the cashier say, "That'll be one million dollars."

And yet Esau was such a lunkhead that he accepted the deal! He was willing to give up his future inheritance to satisfy his present hunger—and Jacob was gleefully willing to take advantage of his brother's fault.

The Blessing Scam

A number of years later, the boys' father, Isaac, came close to death. In his last days, he wanted to pass on the traditional blessing to his oldest son, Esau. This was an important moment; Isaac intended to release his leadership of the clan and pass it on to Esau, who would become the new chief. Isaac asked Esau to go hunt some game and prepare a nice meal in honor of that transfer.

The only problem was that Rebekah, Isaac's wife, overheard the conversation between father and son. And while Isaac viewed Esau as his favorite son because he loved grilled meat, Jacob was Rebekah's favorite because he'd always stayed among the tents and kept her company. Therefore, Rebekah informed Jacob of what was about to happen, and together they came up with a plan to trick Isaac into blessing Jacob rather than Esau. (Was this family tailor-made for reality TV or what?)

Now, Isaac had gone blind in his old age, but he still had his other senses intact. In order to pull the wool over his eyes, so to speak, Rebekah and Jacob used, well, wool. They attached animal pelts to Jacob's arms and neck (because Esau was a hairy man) and dressed him in Esau's finest clothes. Then Rebekah made Isaac's favorite meal, complete with plenty of wine.

When Jacob brought the meal to his father, he

said: "I am Esau your firstborn. I have done as you told me. Please sit up and eat some of my game, so that you may give me your blessing."[25] Scoundrel! Isaac was suspicious at first. But when he touched Jacob's hairy arms and smelled the scent of Esau's clothes, he became convinced. He unknowingly bestowed the family blessing on Jacob, rather than Esau.

When Esau found out about his brother's treachery, he was understandably upset. In fact, he decided to kill Jacob. But Rebekah found out about the whole thing while Esau was still putting together his plan, and she asked Isaac to send Jacob away so that he could find a wife among other descendants of Abraham who lived hundreds of miles away in a place called Haran. (You know how good mothers are at killing two birds with one stone.)

So Jacob had gained his brother's birthright and blessing, but he was forced to leave his home and start a new life in a new place. He stayed in Haran for twenty years, and in those decades he met God for the first time, was deceived several times by someone more sinister than himself, and returned home a genuinely changed man.

Jacob and Esau were ultimately able to set aside their differences and live in peace as adults. Unfortunately, however, their descendants—the nations of Israel and Edom—became bitter enemies as time went on.

Key Bible Passage to Remember

"If I have found favor in your eyes, accept this gift from me. For to see your face is like seeing the face of God, now that you have received me favorably."
(Genesis 33:10)

This verse records the moment when Jacob and Esau experienced reconciliation after being apart for more than twenty years. The restoration of their relationship points to the time when all humanity was given the opportunity to experience reconciliation with God through the death and resurrection of Jesus Christ.

From the Pits to the Palace

Joseph and His Rise in Egypt
(Genesis 37:1–41:57)

Jacob married two women, Leah and Rachel, and had eleven sons and one daughter, but only the youngest son, Joseph, was born to Rachel. (Rachel also had another son, Benjamin, who was not born until after the events of this story.) And since Joseph was the only son of Jacob's favorite wife, he became Jacob's favorite son—much to the chagrin of the others.

Brother for Sale

We don't know a lot about Joseph's early life, but we can put our finger on at least two details. First, Joseph was spoiled by his father, Jacob. The text says Jacob made an ornate robe for Joseph, which was a big deal. Expensive clothing was rare and hard to come by in those days (Nordstrom hadn't been founded yet, after all), so Jacob gave his youngest son a fancy robe (the inspiration for the musical *Joseph and the Amazing Technicolor Dreamcoat*), which was a tangible sign of his favor toward the boy.

And Joseph's older brothers noticed: "When his brothers saw that their father loved him more than any of them, they hated him and could not speak a kind word to him."[26] Things didn't get any better when Joseph brought his father a bad report about his brothers' work habits in the shepherding vocation—in other words, Joseph tattled on them for being lazy.

The second thing we know about Joseph is that his spoiled status went to his head. At the age of seventeen, he received a vision from God concerning the future. Specifically, he had two dreams in which his entire family—including his father and mother—bowed down and paid homage to him. Any sensible young man would have kept this information to himself, but not Joseph. He candidly shared the vision with his brothers and father. Needless to say, it didn't go over well with any of them.

Everything came to a head one day when Joseph was again sent into the fields to check on his brothers. They saw him coming from a long way off—probably because of his colorful robe, ironically—and they decided to take care of him once and for all. Several of the brothers wanted to kill him, but Reuben, the oldest, persuaded the others to throw the boy into a dried-up well so they could take their time deciding what to do with him.

Reuben actually planned to rescue Joseph when his brothers were off working somewhere else, but his plan fell through when a caravan of traders rolled by on their way to Egypt. The brothers decided to sell Joseph as a slave and pocket the money rather than take his life. "After all, he is our brother, our own flesh and blood," they said.[27]

To cover up their illicit agreement, they told their father that Joseph had been attacked and killed by animals. They rubbed Joseph's robe in the blood of a goat and presented it to Jacob in order to give credibility to their deception.

An Offer You Better Refuse

Joseph was taken to Egypt, where he was purchased as a slave by a man named Potiphar, who was the captain of the guard for the pharaoh—the king of Egypt. Joseph apparently learned some lessons about humility during the trip to Egypt, because he kept his head down and worked hard in his new role. More important, Joseph reestablished his relationship with God. As a result, he did well. In fact, Joseph became such a diligent worker and God blessed him so much that "Potiphar put him in charge of his household, and he entrusted to his care everything he owned."[28]

Things were looking up for Joseph, but there was

one major problem: Joseph was a handsome young man, and Potiphar's wife was an amorous old cougar. She propositioned Joseph on several occasions, and each time he refused, unwilling to compromise his integrity. One day when Potiphar was out of town, his wife cornered Joseph in the house, latched on to his cloak, and wouldn't take no for an answer. Joseph had to duck out of his coat and literally run away from the house in order to escape.

Unfortunately, this changed Potiphar's wife from a would-be lover to a woman scorned, and she falsely accused Joseph of trying to rape her—using his cloak as evidence. When Potiphar came home and heard her story, he threw Joseph into the pharaoh's jail.

Joseph once again found himself at the bottom of the barrel. But God was still with him, and Joseph prospered even in prison. He became the right-hand man of the prison warden and assisted in the care of the other prisoners. In that capacity, Joseph came across two men who had once been part of the pharaoh's court—as cupbearer and baker—but were thrown in jail for offending the monarch.

One night, both the cupbearer and the baker had troubling dreams, and they relayed them to Joseph the following morning. With God's help, Joseph recognized that the dreams were visions of the future— just like the ones he'd had when he was seventeen— and he was able to interpret those visions: the cupbearer would return to the pharaoh's service, but the baker would be put to death. And that's exactly what happened a short time later.

Dream with a Happy Ending

After a while, the pharaoh himself was troubled with a similar set of dreams, and no one in his court could help him understand what they meant. That's when the pharaoh's cupbearer remembered his own dreams and that Joseph was able to interpret them. Joseph was taken out of prison and brought before the pharaoh.

He didn't disappoint the king. Under God's direction, Joseph made it clear that the pharaoh's dreams predicted seven years of extreme prosperity in Egypt followed by seven years of extreme famine. Joseph recommended that the pharaoh find someone to manage the country's resources during the successful years so that everyone would have food and seed during the years of starvation. Because the pharaoh could see something special in the young man, he gave the job to Joseph.

In the end, Joseph became second in command over all of Egypt, and his wise plans saved many people from dying of starvation—including his own family.

Key Bible Passage to Remember

"But Joseph said to them, 'Don't be afraid. Am I in the place of God? You intended to harm me, but God intended it for good to accomplish what is now being done, the saving of many lives.'" (*Genesis 50:19–20*)

Joseph spoke these words to his brothers after they were reunited in Egypt. They affirm that the trials in our lives are sometimes part of God's plan to bless the world and bring about reconciliation.

Let My People Go!

Moses and the Exodus
(Exodus 4:18–14:31)

Here's a tough question: How do you convince people to do something they really don't want to do? That's not a problem if you're a Jedi like Obi-Wan Kenobi— you can just use the Force to play mind tricks on unsuspecting individuals. Or, if you're a military hero like William Wallace, all you need is a rousing speech to get people to come over to your way of thinking.

In the book of Exodus, God gave Moses the difficult task of leading the Israelites out of the land of Egypt—where they'd been forced to serve as slaves for hundreds of years—and into the land God had promised to them. The biggest obstacle preventing that from happening was the pharaoh, the king of Egypt, who didn't like the idea of losing a source of free labor as large as the Israelites.

Moses didn't have any fancy words or Jedi mind

tricks up his sleeve that would convince the pharaoh to release the Israelites, but he did have something much better—he was backed by the power and authority of God.

Ten Convincing Arguments

To be fair, Moses tried to be reasonable at the beginning. Accompanied by his brother, Aaron, Moses set up a meet-and-greet with the pharaoh and his advisers during which he attempted to explain the situation. God had commanded Moses to lead the Israelites out of Egypt, so what choice did Moses or anyone else have in the matter?

But the pharaoh didn't see things that way. In fact, he was so offended by Moses's request that he decided to punish all the Israelites working in the land. He decreed that the Israelites would no longer be given the straw needed for making bricks: they would have to gather it themselves. Still, they would be responsible for making the same number of bricks each day. In other words, the pharaoh doubled their workload as a punishment for Moses's insolence.

That's when God, working through Moses and Aaron, decided to play hardball. Over the next several weeks, He sent a series of natural disasters (also called plagues) to the Egyptian community in order to show the pharaoh that He, God, was ultimately in charge.

For the first plague, Moses told Aaron to dip the end of his staff into the Nile River. When he did so, the water of the river turned into blood. All the fish and animals in the Nile died, and the Egyptians were forced to dig wells along the shore of the river in order to get clean drinking water from the ground. But the pharaoh hardened his heart and refused to let the Israelites go free.

The second plague involved huge numbers of frogs swarming over the land of Egypt—even in the people's houses. The third plague involved a multitude of gnats that settled on the people and animals like clouds of dust. The fourth plague was a little different. It involved great swarms of flies that descended on all of Egypt—but there were no flies in the territory called Goshen, which is where the Israelites lived. God was making His point about who had the power.

After the fourth plague, the pharaoh said he would allow the Israelites to go free if Moses would pray to God for the flies to disperse. Moses did pray, and the flies did leave—but the pharaoh hardened his heart again and refused to allow the Israelites to go where they wanted.

God turned things up a notch with the fifth plague. He sent a disease that killed most of the livestock belonging to the Egyptians, but not one animal belonging to the Israelites perished. The sixth plague afflicted the Egyptian people—they became covered in "festering boils."[29] For the seventh plague, God sent a terrible hailstorm that destroyed most of the crops in Egypt (but not in Goshen).

When the pharaoh summoned Moses after the seventh plague, he confessed that he had sinned against God and promised to allow the Israelites to leave if God would stop the hailstorm. Moses prayed, the hail stopped, but the pharaoh once again went back on his word. This guy really couldn't take a hint.

For the eighth plague, God brought an east wind that carried with it a horde of locusts. The bugs descended on every square inch of Egyptian soil and devoured any piece of green that had been left by the hailstorm. Once again the pharaoh summoned Moses, promised to let the Israelites leave, and broke his promise after the locusts were gone.

The ninth plague brought darkness over the land of Egypt for three days. This was an important proof of God's authority because the main deity worshipped by the Egyptians was Ra, the sun god. Even so, the pharaoh still refused to let the Israelites leave on their terms. The tenth plague was the worst of them all. At about midnight, God passed through the households of the Egyptians and took the life of every firstborn child—including the firstborn of the pharaoh.

Parting Company

After the tenth plague, the pharaoh finally had enough. He summoned Moses and ordered him to take the Israelites and leave Egypt as soon as possible. The Egyptian people were so glad to see them go that they actually gave away their prized possessions for the asking in an effort to make the Israelites leave more quickly.

The Israelites were already packed, and they didn't waste much time saying good-bye. They left and set course for the land God had promised them.

After a few days, however, the pharaoh had another change of heart. This seems surprising, but we're talking about a guy who ignored *nine* plagues. He couldn't bear to part with so many hardworking slaves, and so he ordered his army to hop in their fastest chariots and chase the Israelites down, which they did. They caught up with the Israelites while God's people were congregated in front of the Red Sea—which, in the pharaoh's mind, meant they were trapped.

God had other plans, however. He miraculously parted the water in the Red Sea, creating a pathway of dry ground leading through the middle of the water. The Israelites used this to cross the sea and arrive safely on the other side. When the Egyptians tried to follow, however, the water returned to its natural course, and all of the pharaoh's army were swept into the water and drowned. Over on the far bank the Israelites had a party—with Miriam, Moses's sister, leading a tambourine band of dancing women, singing about the horses and riders being thrown into the sea.

Key Bible Passage to Remember

"The blood will be a sign for you on the houses where you are, and when I see the blood, I will pass over you. No destructive plague will touch you when I strike Egypt." (Exodus 12:13)

These instructions were connected with the tenth and final plague. The Israelites were commanded to paint lamb's blood on their doors in order to distinguish themselves from the Egyptians—and God's wrath passed over any house on which He saw the blood. This is a powerful foreshadowing of Jesus's death on the cross, during which His blood was shed so that God's wrath would pass over all who believe in Him.

Three Hundred Good Men

Gideon and the Midianites (Judges 6:1–7:25)

At the Battle of Thermopylae in 480 BCE, King Leonidas and a small force of Greek soldiers held the mighty Persian army at bay for several days. The battle was recently made famous by the movie *300*—a gritty, violent film that pioneered several special-effects techniques. (The film also made Gerard Butler a star, but we shouldn't hold that against it.)

What many people don't realize is that a similar story exists in the Old Testament. More than five hundred years before the Battle of Thermopylae, a young man named Gideon led another army of only three hundred men against one of the most powerful military forces on earth at the time.

Can you guess who won?

A Reluctant Warrior

Don't draw any parallels between Gideon and the Spartan ab workout in the movie, however. Gideon wasn't a career soldier; he wasn't even a man of courage before God got hold of him. In fact, the first thing we read about him in the text is that the angel of the Lord found him while he was threshing grain at the bottom of a winepress—because he was afraid of being discovered by the Midianite army.

Perhaps a bit ironically, the angel greeted Gideon by saying, "The Lord is with you, mighty warrior."[30] Then when the angel informed Gideon that God wanted to use him to help the Israelites break free from the oppressive hand of the Midianites, Gideon again underwhelms: "How can I save Israel?" he asked. "My clan is the weakest in Manasseh, and I am the least in my family."[31]

After using some pyrotechnics to convince Gideon that God really had called him, the angel gave Gideon some unusual instructions: "Tear down your father's altar to Baal and cut down the Asherah pole beside it," he said. "Then build a proper kind of altar to the Lord your God on the top of this height."[32]

Gideon obeyed God, but he destroyed the false idols at night so that nobody would see him. And in the morning, when the townspeople wanted to kill him for his actions, Gideon's father had to stand up for him by saying, "If Baal really is a god, he can defend himself when someone breaks down his altar."[33]

All in all, Gideon was not the ideal man to lead his family into battle, let alone an army. Something happened to him that changed everything, however. The text says, "Then the Spirit of the Lord came on Gideon."[34] Suffused with and supported by the power of God, Gideon turned from a reluctant warrior to a mighty man indeed.

The One-Percent Factor

In time, God called Gideon to raise an army and take a stand against persecution from the Midian- ites and Amalekites—nations that had joined forces to humiliate and eventually eliminate the people of Israel. Gideon responded, gathering together more than thirty thousand men willing to fight. That was a large army for Israel at the time, but Gideon's force was still woefully outnumbered by the Midianites.

It got worse, though. God spoke to Gideon and said, "You have too many men. I cannot deliver Mid- ian into their hands, or Israel would boast against me, 'My own strength has saved me.'"[35] So God in- structed Gideon to tell any soldiers who felt afraid to go home. As a result, twenty-two thousand men abandoned the army—more than two-thirds of Gide- on's forces. (Understandable, since their foes' num- bers were overwhelming.)

It got worse again. God told Gideon that he *still* had too many men. He told Gideon to take the remaining men down to water and watch them drink. Any man who knelt down and put his face directly into the water was sent home, while the men who scooped water into their hands and lapped it up were allowed to stay.

When the winnowing was over, Gideon had an "army" of only three hundred men, just one percent of the original fighting force! And that's when God decided Gideon and his men were ready to attack. Now we're in miracle territory. (God obviously wanted to keep Gideon humble and dependent.)

The Torch Is Mightier Than the Sword

In the middle of the night, Gideon and his three hundred soldiers quietly surrounded the camp of the enemy armies. Each of Gideon's men carried a trumpet and an empty jar with a torch inside it. At a signal from their leader, the men blew their trumpets and smashed the jars on the ground. They held their torches high and cried, "A sword for the Lord and for Gideon!"[36]

Instantly, the camp of the Midianites and Amalekites was transformed into a chaotic mess. The invading armies thought they were being attacked by a superior force, and they began lashing out against anyone they saw in the darkness—which always turned out to be soldiers from their own army, of course. The Midianites and Amalekites spent a period of time zealously killing one another in confusion, and then the survivors fled back home.

Soon after, Gideon roused the people of Israel and assembled a larger army. The Israelites pursued their enemies and won a great victory, breaking free from the oppression of the Midianites and even reclaiming territory that had been lost.

In the end, the Israelites remembered that nothing is impossible when God engineers and supports the effort. And no person is useless in God's hands—even a weak and reluctant warrior like Gideon.

Key Bible Passage to Remember

"The Lord turned to him and said, 'Go in the strength you have and save Israel out of Midian's hand. Am I not sending you?'" (*Judges 6:14*)

The intriguing thing about Gideon's story is that Gideon was a poor choice to become a military leader. He was continually motivated by fear and doubt, and yet he was used by God to accomplish incredible things. Best of all, the same can be true of ordinary people like us.

The World's Worst Haircut

Samson and Delilah
(Judges 16:1–31)

People in today's society are obsessed with superheroes. The Avengers, the X-Men, Superman, Wonder Woman, Spider-Man, Batman, the Flash, the Green Lantern, the Incredibles—we can't get enough stories about men and women who use their extraordinary abilities to fight for truth and justice against the forces of evil.

Maybe that's why Samson is one of the most popular characters in the Bible. And maybe that's why we don't often notice the almost complete waste he made of his life.

Strong but Flawed

Samson was born during a time when the Israelites, God's chosen people, were being oppressed by a neighboring culture called the Philistines. Samson was an Israelite himself, and God set him apart at an early age to help liberate His people from the Philistines (just as Moses had helped liberate His people from the Egyptians).

In order to help Samson accomplish this task, God blessed him with a supernatural amount of physical power. In other words, Samson was really, really strong. Part of Samson's strength was tied to a special vow he made when he was young. He promised never to touch grapes or drink wine, never to touch a dead body, and never to cut his hair—all of which were symbolic of his being set apart for special service to God.

The problem was that Samson had a hard time focusing on his divine mission—and his vow. He broke the first two promises to God when he wandered into a vineyard, touching grapes as he went, and scooped some honey out of a honeycomb constructed in the carcass of a lion, touching its dead body in the process. He also had a strong attraction to Philistine women and ended up marrying one, even though he was supposed to be fighting against the Philistine men.

Because of these flaws, God often had to work through Samson in spite of his selfish nature. When Samson got into a dispute with the family of his Philistine wife, for example, he responded by somehow rounding up three hundred foxes, tying them tail to tail in pairs, fastening a torch to each pair, lighting the torches on fire, and setting the foxes loose in the middle of the Philistines' standing grain. (Talk about being crazy like a fox!)

When a Philistine army came to capture Samson and punish him for his handiwork, Samson grabbed the jawbone of a donkey and fought against them— one man against thousands. By the time the dust settled, Samson had killed more than a thousand Philistine soldiers.

So God found a way to use Samson to accomplish His purposes in spite of Samson's very noticeable flaws and his self-centered nature.

You Don't Love Me Anymore

Things went on that way for quite a while until something seemingly unimaginable happened to Samson: he fell in love. Specifically, he fell in love with a Philistine woman named Delilah. Even more specifically, he fell in love with a Philistine woman named Delilah who didn't have any reciprocal feelings for him. That being the case, when the Philistine leaders approached Delilah and offered her a boatload of money to uncover the secret source of Samson's supernatural strength, she accepted.

A short time later, Delilah cooed and batted her eyelashes at Samson as she said, "Tell me the secret of your great strength and how you can be tied up and subdued." (Apparently, subtlety wasn't her strong suit.) Samson answered with a lie, claiming that he would become as weak as any other man if he were tied up with seven fresh bowstrings that had never been tied.

Later that night, Delilah woke him up by yelling, "The Philistines are upon you!" Coincidentally, when he came to his senses, he noticed that seven fresh bowstrings had been tied around his body. He snapped them as though they were toothpicks and went on his way.

The days that followed cycled through a similar pattern of events. Delilah kept pressing Samson about the source of his great strength. Samson kept giving her bogus answers. And Delilah kept attempting to subdue Samson based on those bogus answers. The situation finally came to a head when Samson could no longer stand her accusations that he didn't love her because he wouldn't tell her the truth about the secret to his strength. Here's what the text says: "With such nagging she prodded him day after day until he was sick to death of it."[37] (Yes, that's a real Bible verse.)

And so, finally, Samson gave up the secret. He told her that his hair had never been cut because of his early vow to God, and that he would lose his power if it were cut at any time in the future.

Sure enough, Delilah cut off his seven braids of hair as he slept that night, and then she called in the Philistine soldiers to capture him. Samson tried to fight back, but his divine strength had left him. The Philistines seized him and gouged out his eyes. Then they took him to Gaza, their capital city, and forced him to grind their grain with what little strength he had left.

Through his own folly, Samson the superhero was brought down and made low.

Bringing Down the House

Some time later, the Philistines put on a huge celebration to worship their god, Dagon. They called for Samson to be brought out as part of the festivities. In fact, one of the saddest verses in the Bible says: "So they called Samson out of the prison, and he performed for them."[38]

But Samson had one more trick up his sleeve. When he was placed between the main pillars of the Philistine temple, he cried out to God for the last time. "Sovereign Lord, remember me," he said. Then he pushed with all his might against the two pillars, and they came crashing down—along with the temple they had been supporting.

So Samson died in one final feat of strength, and three thousand of the Philistines died with him. He came through with one last superhero feat for the Lord.

Key Bible Passage to Remember

"A certain man of Zorah, named Manoah, from the clan of the Danites, had a wife who was childless, unable to give birth. The angel of the Lord appeared to her and said, 'You are barren and childless, but you are going to become pregnant and give birth to a son.'" (Judges 13:2–3)

An angel of God visited Samson's parents to proclaim the birth of their son, who would deliver the Israelites from the Philistines. This event foreshadows the visit Mary received from a similar angel, who proclaimed that Jesus would be born and deliver His people from their sins.

Shepherd Boy with a Slingshot

David and Goliath
(1 Samuel 17:1–58)

King David is one of the most famous people in the Bible. He fought in wars. He wrote amazing songs. He had a very public (and very damaging) affair with a woman named Bathsheba. Most important of all, he was an ancestor of Jesus Christ.

But before he became king, David was the eighth and youngest son of a shepherding family—an insignificant boy from an insignificant town in an insignificant country called Israel. But his fame blossomed when he found himself in a fight for his life against one of the most famous (and most feared) warriors in history.

A Giant-Size Problem

During the reign of Israel's first king, Saul—about three hundred years after Samson and Delilah walked the earth—the Philistines once again gathered their armies in order to attack the Israelites. The two nations had been enemies for centuries, but now the Philistines had an ace up their collective sleeve—a super-soldier named Goliath.

Goliath was a formidable enemy, and he struck fear into the hearts of even the bravest soldiers who came against him. That wasn't because he had ninja skills, or even supernatural strength like Samson's. It's because he was really, really big. The Bible says, "His height was six cubits and a span."[39] If you don't have your ancient-world conversion charts handy, I'll spare you the trouble of finding them—Goliath was nine feet nine inches tall. He wasn't a beanpole, either. His bronze armor alone weighed 125 pounds. (Think of André the Giant in *The Princess Bride* movie, then add another twenty-five inches and a couple hundred pounds!)

Goliath was also mean as a snake. It was his custom to stand in front of the Israelite army every morning and every evening and challenge someone to come and face him in a fight. Not surprisingly, nobody ever did.

Nobody until David, that is.

Strutting His Stuff

As mentioned earlier, David was the youngest son in a shepherding family, which meant he stayed at home to watch the sheep when all his older brothers went off to fight the Philistines. But David wasn't totally separated from the battle. One day his father told him to carry some food and other provisions to the front lines and deliver them to his brothers.

David arrived at the encampment just as Goliath starting walking in front of the Israelite army, shouting his taunts and challenges. Naturally, David wanted to know what was going on. And despite the fact that David's oldest brother was irritated with him for leaving the sheep, he got some answers: "Now the Israelites had been saying, 'Do you see how this man keeps coming out? He comes out to defy Israel. The king will give great wealth to the man who kills him. He will also give him his daughter in marriage and will exempt his family from taxes in Israel.'"[40]

What's interesting about David is that he wasn't impressed by the offer of great wealth or a princess as a wife. Rather, David became angry because of the way Goliath was disrespecting God and God's people. He asked, "Who is this uncircumcised Philistine that he should defy the armies of the living God?"[41] And he must have been pretty vocal about his displeasure, because before long he was summoned to appear before King Saul.

David didn't back down in the presence of the king. In fact, since nobody seemed willing to fight the giant, David offered to do it himself. Saul was initially skeptical, of course, but David described some of his exploits as a shepherd—he'd managed to kill both a lion and a bear with only his hands. But it was David's unshakable faith that convinced Saul to take a chance on him. David said: "The Lord who rescued me from the paw of the lion and the paw of the bear will rescue me from the hand of this Philistine."[42]

And that's how David found himself walking onto the field of battle, planning to intentionally provoke a giant into a fight for his life.

The Bigger They Are . . .

Saul initially tried to clothe David in his own battle dress, including a coat of armor and a bronze helmet. But David wasn't used to such adornments, and he preferred to face the giant with nothing more than his staff and his sling. The only new weaponry he took with him were five smooth stones that he picked up from a nearby stream as he approached the Philistines.

When Goliath saw the boy coming, he scoffed. "Am I a dog," he said, "that you come at me with sticks?"[43] David answered Goliath's taunt: "This day the Lord will deliver you into my hands, and I'll strike you down and cut off your head."[44] Take that!

And with that, the fight was on—although it wasn't a very long fight. As Goliath, like an over-dressed bull, gathered himself and prepared to charge the boy, David raced in toward him and fired a stone from his sling. The rock hit Goliath in the head, but it didn't bounce off; it sunk into the giant's skull, killing him instantly. Then David grabbed Goliath's own sword and fulfilled his promise by cutting off the giant's head.

David's actions did wonders for the morale of the Israelite army. Suddenly feeling more courageous, they charged their enemies and struck them down, pursuing the opposing army all the way back to the Philistines' main city.

It was quite a day for the Israelites and quite an accomplishment for David—the shepherd boy who would one day become one of the greatest and most famous kings in history.

Key Bible Passage to Remember

"David said to the Philistine, 'You come against me with sword and spear and javelin, but I come against you in the name of the Lord Almighty, the God of the armies of Israel, whom you have defied.'" (1 Samuel 17:45)

God used David to turn the known world upside down and catapult the nation of Israel, God's chosen people, into prominence. David's story effectively foreshadows that of his descendant Jesus Christ, whose actions on earth changed the course of history.

Whose God Wins?

Elijah and the Prophets of Baal
(1 Kings 18:16–40)

Today we have a variety of methods we can use when we need to make a choice between two options that seem attractive. "Eeny meeny miny mo" is probably the most commonly used. Or maybe flipping a coin. There's also rock-paper-scissors, if two people are involved. And if there are a lot of people who need to make a choice, we can go democratic and vote on it.

Several thousand years ago, the inhabitants of ancient Israel needed to make a choice between God, the One who'd saved and sustained them for years, and another god who influenced them from foreign lands called Baal. The prophet Elijah helped them make that choice—not through rock-paper-scissors but by setting up a test that was as brutal as it was straightforward.

Eight Hundred Fifty Prophets to One

After David and Solomon, the ancient Israelites didn't have much luck when it came to kings. The men (and a few women) who ruled the nation had a tendency to abandon God and turn to idol worship instead—apparently, statues made of gold and wood were much easier to control than the Creator of the universe. Unfortunately, the people of Israel usually followed the lead of their king, who often attributed the flashy success of his military exploits or his abundance of material wealth to the influence of these gods. For this reason, the people usually wound up fashioning idols or shrines in the gods' honor.

King Ahab of Israel was a ruler who wanted to avoid his own nation's God; rather, he much preferred the cult god Baal, worshipped by his foreign wife, Jezebel. Baal was supposed to be especially good at producing plentiful crops and was known as a fertility god. Now, the bane of Ahab's existence was a rough-and-tumble man named Elijah. He was a most powerful prophet of God, and he regularly warned the people about the evil and ensuing consequences of following the path taken by Ahab and his wife.

Usually Elijah remained in hiding (because defying a king isn't good for your life expectancy), but one day the prophet appeared before Ahab's court and gave the king a direct order: "Now summon the people from all over Israel to meet me on Mount Carmel. And bring the four hundred and fifty prophets of Baal and the four hundred prophets of Asherah, who eat at Jezebel's table."[45]

Maybe Ahab was curious as to what Elijah was up to. Maybe he hoped God's servant was ready to join the prophets of Baal and Asherah. Maybe he simply respected a man who didn't cower down before him. Whatever the reason, Ahab acquiesced to Elijah's request and had the people of Israel assemble on the mountain known as Carmel.

Once everyone arrived, Elijah got straight to the point: "How long will you waver between two opinions?" he asked the people. "If the Lord is God, follow him; but if Baal is God, follow him."[46] The people of Israel didn't answer. They weren't ready to defy the king—or the king's wife.

So Elijah issued a challenge. He proposed that the people slaughter two bulls as a sacrifice, and have them placed upon two altars—one for Elijah, and the other for the prophets of Asherah and Baal. Elijah told the people not to set fire to the sacrifices, however. "[Y]ou call on the name of your god, and I will call on the name of the Lord," he said. "The god who answers by fire—he is God."[47]

The people thought it was a great idea, and they prepared everything just as Elijah said.

Time to Bail on Baal

Elijah was a good sport, so he allowed the prophets of Asherah and Baal to go first. And they went for it with gusto. From morning until noon the prophets called out to their gods—but no fire.

At noon, Elijah started to contribute some encouraging words. "Shout louder!" he said. "Surely he is a god! Perhaps he is deep in thought, or busy, or traveling. Maybe he is sleeping and must be awakened."[48] (He was even crass enough to suggest that Baal might be using the bathroom!) The prophets of Asherah and Baal shouted louder. They self-mutilated, cutting themselves with swords. They screamed and danced wildly around the sacrifice, looking like a bunch of clowns. But the text says, "[T]here was no response, no one answered, no one paid attention."[49]

When evening came, Elijah gathered twelve large stones and built his own altar. He laid the wood on top of the stones and placed one of the bulls on top of the wood. Then he dug a trench around the whole altar. Then he said something crazy: "Fill four large jars with water and pour it on the offering and on the wood."[50] The people were confused, but they did as he asked. Then he said to pour the water again. They did. Then Elijah said to do it a third time, and afterward the water ran down the altar and filled up the trench Elijah had dug.

Then the prophet prayed. Rather than shriek-ing or wounding himself, he said, "Lord, the God of Abraham, Isaac and Israel, let it be known today that you are God in Israel and that I am your servant and have done all these things at your command."[51] God answered in a big way.

All Fired Up

Fire came crashing down from heaven and engulfed the altar, burning up both the wood and the bull. It also burned off all the water running through the rocks and completely dried out the water-filled trench. The people fell on their faces, thinking this was awesome. "The Lord—he is God!" they cried. "The Lord—he is God!"[52]

Never one to miss an opportunity, Elijah or-dered the people to capture the false prophets of Asherah and Baal—and to slaughter them. The people obeyed. Those who had led Israel away from their God were brought down to the Kishon Valley and killed because they led the people into wickedness.

Once and for all, God had shown His people what was real and what was make-believe. He'd shown them that He alone was worthy of worship and thanksgiving; that He was responsible for their harvests and many blessings.

Key Bible Passage to Remember

"Answer me, Lord, answer me, so these people will know that you, Lord, are God, and that you are turning their hearts back again" (1 Kings 18:37)

If it seems harsh for Elijah to have ordered the deaths of more than eight hundred people, it was. It was a terrible day. But it was also necessary. The false prophets had intentionally led the people of Israel down a path of spiritual ruin, and if they didn't face judgment the people of Israel would have faced judgment in even larger numbers.

Part-Time Prophet, Part-Time Lion Tamer

Daniel and the Lions' Den
(Daniel 6:1–28)

One of the most interesting things about the Bible is that most of the people who appear in its pages are noticeably flawed. Abraham was a man of great faith, for example, but he still disobeyed God by sleeping with his wife's maidservant in order to have a son. Similarly, Moses knew God well enough to speak with Him face-to-face, but he still committed murder in his early years. The stories recorded in God's Word ring true because they involve real people making real mistakes—just like us.

Every now and then, however, people came along who really did live saintly lives—people who stood against evil and were faithful to God from beginning to end. And of those people, Daniel was probably one of the most outstanding.

Of the Best and Brightest

Daniel was a young man when Nebuchadnezzar and the Babylonians conquered Jerusalem. In those days it was common for a victorious army to capture the best and brightest people from a defeated nation and bring them back to their own land—a practice that strengthened the conquerors and weakened the conquered.

That's how Daniel found himself a member of the upper class in Babylon. Fortunately for Daniel, he was a highly adaptable thinker and distinguished himself with his wisdom even as a young person. In fact, he became a trusted adviser to King Nebuchadnezzar and one of the most powerful men in the kingdom—he also helped out the king's son, Belshazzar, when he replaced his father on the throne.

In other words, though Daniel started out as a captive, he made a pretty nice life for himself in Babylon, just as Joseph did in Egypt. That's why it must have seemed like a bad thing when another army—an alliance between the Medes and the Persians—conquered the Babylonians and took control of their empire.

But it wasn't a bad thing. Daniel was such an exceptional person that he quickly became a favorite of the new king—a man named Darius. Unfortunately, the other people in Darius's coterie weren't willing to tolerate any new competition on their turf.

Between a Lion and a Hard Place

King Darius was evidently a big fan of org charts; he appointed 120 leaders, called satraps, who were given authority to rule throughout the different regions of his empire. Darius also appointed three administrators to take charge of the satraps and hold them accountable. It was a pretty clever system, which ensured that Darius didn't have to be bothered with a lot of details—and that someone could always be held accountable if something went wrong.

Daniel was one of the three administrators appointed to manage the satraps, and he was good at his job. Actually, he was more than good; he was phenomenal. The text says: "Daniel so distinguished himself among the administrators and the satraps by his exceptional qualities that the king planned to set him over the whole kingdom."[53]

Remember, though, that Daniel was an outsider. He was a Jew who'd been taken captive by the Babylonians—and then taken captive again by the Medes and Persians. So having Daniel in charge didn't sit well with some of the satraps. And it certainly didn't sit well with the other two administrators. Therefore, Daniel's enemies conspired to get him kicked out of office.

There was just one problem: Daniel was squeaky clean. He had no skeletons (or Monicas) in his closet. He was as honest as he was hardworking, and his integrity was unmatched—it was kind of like trying to attack Mother Teresa or Gandhi.

The satraps and administrators came up with a new plan. They knew Daniel was still faithful to God, so they convinced King Darius to sign a law stating that, for thirty days, any person who prayed to any god or human being other than the king would be thrown into a den of lions.

When Daniel heard about the new law, he had a choice to make: obey the law written by his king or obey God. According to the text, Daniel didn't hesitate for a second: "Now when Daniel learned that the decree had been published, he went home to his upstairs room where the windows opened toward Jerusalem. Three times a day he got down on his knees and prayed, giving thanks to his God, just as he had done before."[54]

Sure enough, the satraps arrested Daniel for breaking the law. And because it was the custom that the laws of the Medes and Persians could not be changed, Darius could do nothing to help his most trusted adviser. He was forced to have his friend thrown into a pit filled with hungry lions, and he was forced to watch as the lid of that pit was sealed tight, allowing no escape.

Only a Pit Stop

It was a long night for Darius. He couldn't eat. He couldn't sleep. He was unimpressed by the different methods of entertainment with which the satraps and administrators tried to distract him. And when morning came, he ran down to the pit. The text says, "[H]e called to Daniel in an anguished voice, 'Daniel, servant of the living God, has your God, whom you serve continually, been able to rescue you from the lions?'"[55]

And Daniel answered! He was alive. When the king pulled him out of the pit, Daniel told his story—God had sent an angel to sit with him during his time in the pit, and the angel had shut the mouths of the lions. Daniel hadn't gotten so much as a scratch.

That wasn't the case for the men who'd manipulated the king, however. Darius had them all thrown into the lions' den that same day, and the text says, "[B]efore they reached the floor of the den, the lions overpowered them and crushed all their bones."[56] These were certainly lions of discriminating tastes! Daniel went on to continue his illustrious career.

Key Bible Passage to Remember

"For he is the living God and he endures forever; his kingdom will not be destroyed, his dominion will never end. He rescues and he saves; he performs signs and wonders in the heavens and on the earth. He has rescued Daniel from the power of the lions." (Daniel 6:26–27)

After Daniel's amazing story, King Darius wrote these words as a proclamation throughout his empire. Daniel's faith and faithfulness resulted in thousands of people hearing the good news that God saves those who trust in Him.

Persia's Supermodel

Queen Esther Saves Israel
(Esther 2:1–7:10)

Are you willing to admit you like reality television? It's okay if you do. Even though a lot of people distance themselves from reality TV or make fun of its constant presence in pop culture, most of us have a guilty pleasure or two stashed away in our DVRs. Maybe it's *American Idol*, for example. Or *Survivor*. Or *America's Next Top Model*. Or *Swamp People*.

Whatever your favorite show (or shows) may be today, the truth is that the first reality competition took place thousands of years ago in Susa, the capital of ancient Persia.

The Twelve-Month Makeovers

It all started at a party thrown by Persia's king, a man named Xerxes. If you've seen *300*, you already know that he was a big fan of partying, and one particular celebration lasted seven whole days. On the seventh day, when everyone was thoroughly inebriated, Xerxes commanded his wife, Vashti, to join the party and "display her beauty" for the other men to see.[57] This wasn't an innocent request. What Xerxes had in mind wasn't the talent portion of the Miss America pageant; it was more like a peep show in Vegas.

Not surprisingly, Vashti refused the king's command. As a result, she was stripped of her position as queen and commanded never to appear in his presence again—not a big loss for her. Xerxes needed a new queen, however, and so his servants scoured the kingdom and found the most "beautiful young virgins"[58] in the land, all of whom were brought to live in the king's harem. Every woman was given a full year of beauty treatments—"six months with oil of myrrh and six with perfumes and cosmetics"[59]—and then allowed to spend one night with the king. He would then choose his favorite and appoint her as the new queen.

See? They just needed cameras and Tyra Banks to turn to the whole thing into a full-blown reality series. What's crazy, though, is that things didn't get *really* interesting until after the competition and the story shifted from reality TV to soap opera.

As the Ancient World Turns

This soap opera has several different characters, but the most important is a young Jewish woman named Esther. It was she who won the competition and replaced Vashti as queen of Persia. Interestingly, she kept her Jewish heritage a secret when she moved into the palace.

The next character is Mordecai, who happened to be Esther's uncle and the man who raised her from a young age after her parents died. Mordecai was one of Xerxes's officials, and he spent much of his time working through civil and political matters in the king's court. Here's another interesting tidbit: after Esther became queen, Mordecai uncovered a plot to assassinate the king. He reported it to Esther and the would-be assassins were captured before they could carry out their nefarious plans.

The villain of the soap opera was a man named Haman. He was also one of the king's officials and, after Esther became queen, he became second in command of the Persian Empire. (Coincidentally, or not, Haman's promotion occurred right after he donated a huge sum of money to the royal treasury.) One last tidbit: Haman was an Agagite—a race of people who had hated the Jews for generations.

Haman's promotion kick-started the main conflict of the story. As the king's right-hand man, Haman expected everyone (except the king) to bow down and pay him homage whenever they saw him. And everyone did—except for Mordecai. Esther's uncle refused to bow, probably because of the ancient feud between Jews and the descendants of Agag, and also because Jews didn't think of their rulers as akin to gods.

Well, Haman wasn't about to take any guff from Mordecai. But instead of getting revenge on the one person who defied him, Haman decided to donate *more* money to the royal coffers in exchange for the king writing a law that allowed Haman to destroy all the Jewish people in Persia on a specific day.

When Mordecai heard about the new law, he tore his robe, dressed in sackcloth and ashes (the traditional ancient garb of someone mourning or repenting), and went about the city wailing loudly because of his misery. (And partly because he was now itchy and dirty.)

She Left Him Hanging

When Esther heard what had happened, she sent a messenger to speak with Mordecai. He explained everything, and he asked the messenger to ask Esther to approach the king and request that he intervene on behalf of her people. But Esther was hesitant to do so at first. She hadn't told anyone she was a Jew, remember, and there was a law in the palace forbidding anyone to approach the king without being summoned—even the queen. Whoever approached the king would be put to death unless the king extended his golden scepter as a gesture of favor.

Esther eventually agreed to do what Mordecai

wanted her to do, and she asked Mordecai and the Jews to join her in three days of fasting and prayer beforehand. When she approached the king, he held out his scepter. Phew! But instead of pleading her case then and there, Esther asked the king to join her for a meal the following day—and to bring Haman with him.

In the meantime, several interesting things happened. First, Haman built a huge set of gallows on which he planned to hang Mordecai and his family when the "death day" for the Jews rolled around. Second, the king had a bout of insomnia that night, and he asked for someone to read from the historical scrolls to help him sleep. Coincidentally, the scrolls contained the account of Mordecai saving the king's life from assassins.

The next morning, Xerxes asked Haman what would make a good celebration for "the man the king delights to honor."[60] Haman thought Xerxes was talking about him, so he listed a whole bunch of awesome rewards. When Haman was done with his list, the king said: "Do just as you have suggested for Mordecai the Jew."[61] Burn!

When he finished honoring Mordecai, his enemy, Haman rushed over to the dinner date he had with Xerxes and Esther. When he arrived, however, Esther told the king about Haman's plot to destroy her people. Double burn! Xerxes was so mad he went out to the balcony to calm down, and Haman threw himself on Esther's lap to beg for mercy. But the king came back in and thought Haman was attempting to assault his wife. Triple burn!

The upshot was that Haman was hanged on the same gallows he had prepared for Mordecai, and King Xerxes wrote a new law that allowed the Jews to defend themselves on the forthcoming "death day"— which they did. In other words, it was a very happy ending!

Key Bible Passage to Remember

"For if you remain silent at this time, relief and deliverance for the Jews will arise from another place, but you and your father's family will perish. And who knows but that you have come to your royal position for such a time as this?"
(Esther 4:14)

The book of Esther is the only book in the Bible that doesn't contain God's name. But these words, spoken by Mordecai when he convinced Esther to intercede with the king, show that God was diligently working behind the scenes to bring about salvation for His people.

A Whale of a Tale

Jonah and the Big Fish
(Jonah 1:1–4:11)

There are several famous fish stories currently swimming around in our cultural lexicon. *Moby-Dick* is probably the best known—who hasn't heard about Captain Ahab's fatal quest to hunt down the white whale? Then there's *Free Willy*, which is a crowd-pleaser, and the *Jaws* franchise, which scared an entire generation of people out of the water.

But there's a biblical story that precedes each of those by thousands of years: the tale of Jonah and the Big Fish.

Wrong-Way Ticket

The Bible doesn't provide a lot of backstory on Jonah—only that he was the son of a man named Amittai, and that he was a "prophet from Gath Hepher."[62] But the book of Jonah does tell us what God commanded Jonah to do: "Go to the great city of

Nineveh and preach against it, because its wickedness has come up before me."[63]

This wasn't an easy assignment. During Jonah's time, Nineveh was one of the greatest cities in the world. It was also one of the more wicked places imaginable—kind of like a cross between the dangerous parts of Los Angeles and the seedier parts of Las Vegas. But preaching God's Word to people who need to hear it is the first item in a prophet's job description, so Jonah hopped on the first boat traveling to Nineveh. Right?

Wrong. Jonah did hop on a boat, but he bought a ticket for Tarshish instead—and Tarshish was located in the exact opposite direction from Nineveh. This wasn't a mistake on Jonah's part. The text tells us he "ran away from the Lord."[64] Unfortunately for Jonah, and for the other people on the ship, the fact that God knows everything makes it hard for people to give Him the slip. God saw what Jonah was up to, and He took a few steps to correct the prophet's intended destination.

A Seventy-Two–Hour Stomachache

The first step came in the form of a massive storm so violent that the professional sailors were deathly afraid. As the wind raged and waves crashed, the seamen called out to their various gods and threw all the cargo overboard in order to lighten the vessel. Amazingly, Jonah wasn't aware of the gravity of the situation because he was hunkered down belowdecks—fast asleep. After they woke him up, the sailors became even more afraid when Jonah told them he was running away from "the God of heaven, who made the sea and the dry land."[65]

The sailors asked what they should do to survive the storm, and Jonah told them plainly enough: "'Pick me up and throw me into the sea,' he replied, 'and it will become calm. I know that it is my fault that this great storm has come upon you.'"[66] The sailors tried everything else they could think of—they even tried to row back to land—but in the end they did what Jonah said.

And the moment God's prophet entered the water, the storm died away and the seas became as smooth as glass.

That wasn't the end of Jonah, however. The second step of God's plan involved a "huge fish"[67] (not specifically designated a whale) that swallowed the prophet whole and carried him down into the depths of the sea. The fish must not have been anything like the one in *Jaws* because, amazingly, Jonah survived being ingested. Even more amazingly, he lived in the stomach of the great fish for three days.

Of course, Jonah didn't have a lot of entertainment options in the fish's belly, which meant he was forced to spend a lot of time thinking about and reevaluating some of his recent decisions. He eventually came to the conclusion that disobeying and running away from an all-knowing and all-powerful God wasn't such a hot idea.

As a result, Jonah confessed his sin and rebellion against God. He acknowledged that God was in control of his situation, and he once again committed to serve as a prophet by proclaiming God's Word to the people who needed to hear it most.

After three days of rather unpleasant living conditions, according to the text, "the Lord commanded the fish, and it vomited Jonah onto dry land."[68]

Countdown to Destruction

After Jonah's little detour, God once again called him to go to "the great city of Nineveh and proclaim to it the message I give you."[69] And wouldn't you know it, this time Jonah obeyed. He traveled toward Nineveh and hiked into the city, a day's journey. Then he proclaimed the message God had given him: "Forty more days and Nineveh will be overthrown."[70] God really had a thing for forty days.

That's when something completely unexpected happened: the Ninevites responded. They recognized the truth of Jonah's message and repented of their sin. In fact, things got so crazy that the king of Nineveh sent out a decree commanding his people to fast and mourn in sackcloth and ashes because of their rebellion against God—and to ask God to spare them from destruction.

God heard. He saw how the people turned away from their wickedness. And, in the same spirit of mercy with which He provided a great fish to rescue His prophet, God spared the people of Nineveh from the destruction they deserved.

Key Bible Passage to Remember

"Those who cling to worthless idols turn away from God's love for them. But I, with shouts of grateful praise, will sacrifice to you. What I have vowed I will make good. I will say, 'Salvation comes from the Lord.'" (Jonah 2:8–9)

These words are among Jonah's reflections while he was in the belly of the great fish. When everything else was stripped away, Jonah was finally able to see the love God had been extending toward him—and he was finally able to realize that God alone can bring salvation.

PART II

The New Testament

The Greatest Story Often Told

The Christmas Story
(Matthew 1:18–2:23; Luke 1:26–2:21)

Is there anything more dramatic and inspiring than a good rescue story? Whether it's the National Guard pulling people from rooftops after Hurricane Katrina or New York City rescue workers risking their lives to search for survivors in the rubble of the World Trade Center after the attacks on 9/11, we love to hear about people being saved when all hope seemed lost.

And that's really the message of the Christmas story. Sin had ravaged humanity ever since the fall of Adam and Eve, so God took matters into His own hands and initiated something new—a divine rescue plan through which we could experience salvation from our sins once and for all.

Virgin Territory

It all started in a tiny village north of Jerusalem called Nazareth. Mary, a young virgin, probably thirteen or fourteen years old, was betrothed to a young carpenter named Joseph. Her wedding plans were interrupted rather abruptly, however, when she received a visit from an angel who had rather surprising news. "Do not be afraid, Mary," said the angel. "You have found favor with God. You will conceive and give birth to a son, and you are to call him Jesus."[71]

Now, this announcement may not have been a total surprise to Mary, since the Old Testament contains several prophecies about the birth of the Messiah. But there was a complication in Mary's situation, and she noticed it right away: "'How will this be,' Mary asked the angel, 'since I am a virgin?'"[72] A reasonable question! The angel's answer was mysterious and frightening and exciting all at the same time. He told her that God's Spirit would "overshadow"[73] her in a supernatural way—which meant that she would conceive the child without her future husband. God Himself would be the Father, and the resulting child would be both fully human and fully divine.

That's exactly what happened—although the whole thing was a bit hard for Joseph to swallow at first. He cared for Mary, and when he concluded the only logical reason for her pregnancy was that she'd been unfaithful to him, he tried to find a way to end their betrothal quietly so that he could spare her as much shame as possible while still obeying the law.

But while he was still trying to figure out his next step, Joseph also received a visit from the angel, this time in a dream. The angel told Joseph that Mary had been faithful to him, and that the child really was a divine gift—a Savior. Fittingly, the angel instructed Joseph to remain by Mary's side and name the child Jesus, which means "the Lord saves."

The Wrong Side of Town

Near the end of Mary's pregnancy, Caesar Augustus ordered a census to be taken throughout the population, which meant that families who were traveling were forced to return to their original homesteads. As a descendent of David, Joseph was required to travel to Bethlehem, the City of David—and to bring a very pregnant Mary with him. When they arrived, the city was so full they were unable to find affordable accommodations. With no other options, Joseph and Mary were forced to lodge in an animal shelter (animals included), which had probably been built into a small cave among the rocks and crags within the city.

It was in that dark, dank, depressing hole that

Jesus Christ—the only hope and true Light of the world—was born.

The miraculous event didn't go unnoticed or uncelebrated, however. God arranged a spectacular birth announcement for His Son, complete with a heavenly light show and an angelic choir. Yet strangely, the only people privileged to see it were a bunch of lowly shepherds sleeping out in the fields with their sheep because they were too poor to afford lodgings for themselves or their animals. "I bring you good news that will cause great joy for all the people," one of the angels told the shepherds. "Today in the town of David a Savior has been born to you; he is the Messiah, the Lord."[74]

Leaving the Scene of the "Crime"

Actually, the shepherds weren't the only ones to receive the news. Thousands of miles away, a group of learned men (called Magi) from the East noticed a significant celestial event in the sky—something indicating the birth of a new and important king. In fact, the sign announced an event so shocking that the men decided they had to see it for themselves.

They loaded up supplies and traveled for at least a year before they reached Jerusalem. When they arrived, they started asking a bunch of questions about the new king who had been born—questions that caught the attention of Herod the Great, who ruled over the province on behalf of the Roman Empire.

Herod spoke with the Magi and instructed them to let him know when they found the new king. He claimed he wanted to worship with them, but really he wanted to destroy any potential competition. Fortunately, after the Magi found Mary and Joseph and presented several gifts to their Son, Jesus, the King, they were warned by God in a dream not to report anything to Herod.

Even more fortunately, Joseph was warned about the situation in another dream; he was instructed to take his new family and flee to Egypt in order to escape Herod's wrath. And wrath did come. When Herod realized the Magi had given him the slip, he was furious, and he ordered the death of every boy in Bethlehem who was two years old and under.

Jesus escaped, of course, but the contrast between him and Herod couldn't be more striking— or more terrible. On the one hand was Herod, a tyrant so twisted by wickedness that he was willing to slaughter innocent children in order to retain political control over a backwater province of the Roman Empire. On the other hand was Jesus, the sinless King of the universe, who came to save us all from our own wickedness and carry us to a new and better future.

Key Bible Passage to Remember

"She will give birth to a son, and you are to give him the name Jesus, because he will save his people from their sins." *(Matthew 1:21)*

These words, spoken by the angel to Joseph, reflect the foundation of the Gospel and the Christian faith—humanity had a problem we couldn't fix, our sin and separation from God, but God Himself came to live among us in order to set us free.

The Life of the Party

Jesus Turns Water into Wine
(John 2:1–12)

Are you a student of oenology? Would you even take things to the next level and describe yourself as an oenophile? No, those terms don't have anything to do with weird religions or some kind of communicable disease. Rather, they refer to wine. Oenology is the study of wine and wine making, and an oenophile is simply someone who loves wine.

There are a lot of oenophiles in today's culture. They buy wines in bottles and cases to add to their collections. They pour wine into fancy glasses so they can see it, swirl it, sniff it, sip it, savor it—and sometimes even swallow it.

But nothing in oenology can explain what happened two thousand years ago, when Jesus performed His first public miracle by briefly stepping into the wine-making business.

No Longer in High Spirits

It all started in Cana, which was a small village located between the Mediterranean and the Sea of Galilee. Two young people in the village were getting married, and Jesus was invited to attend, along with His disciples. Jesus's mother, Mary, was also invited, and they all attended the happy occasion.

Weddings are a big deal in today's culture—they require a lot of planning (and usually a lot of money) to pull off. The same was true in the ancient world, although the social importance of a wedding celebration was much greater. There weren't a lot of social opportunities back then, which meant that everyone in the community became legitimately excited when a young man and woman decided to tie the knot, because it gave everyone a rare opportunity to get together.

That's why what happened at this particular wedding in Cana was so scandalous: "When the wine was gone, Jesus's mother said to him, 'They have no more wine.'"[75] Okay, maybe that's not a situation you would have found on *Desperate Housewives*, but it was a *huge* deal in the ancient world. Hospitality was vitally important in everyday life, and people who hosted a party had a social obligation to provide their guests with a good time, a time of joy and celebration—and nothing said joy and celebration in those days better than fine wine. So running out of wine was an extremely embarrassing situation for the host family. It would have been viewed as offensive by the guests, and it may even have reflected poorly on the prospects of marital happiness for the bride and groom.

A Jarring Effect

Mary must have had a close relationship with the host family, because she made a point of alerting Jesus to the situation. She wasn't telling Him about the lack of wine because she was thirsty, in other words. She wanted Him to do something about it to help out the family and the newlyweds.

Jesus was hesitant at first. "Woman, why do you involve me?" He asked. "My hour has not yet come." By saying, "My hour has not yet come,"[76] Jesus meant it wasn't yet time for Him to reveal Himself publicly as the Messiah—as the Savior. Such a revelation would launch Him inevitably toward His death, and it wasn't the right moment for Him to start walking down that road.

Mary commanded the house servants to "Do whatever he tells you," referring to Jesus. This was her way of getting Jesus involved without exposing His identity—you know how mothers are good at getting you to do things you don't really want to do. You just can't say no to Mom.

So Jesus got involved for the sake of His mom.

He pointed to six stone jars and told the servants to fill them with water. The jars were normally used for ceremonial washing, and each one held between twenty and thirty gallons—a lot of water, strictly speaking. The servants did what Jesus asked, filling the jars to the brim.

What happened next was a bit crazy: "Then he told them, 'Now draw some out and take it to the master of the banquet.'"[77] Remember, these jars were normally used for washing people; they probably held the water and rags used to wash guests' feet as they entered the house. So they weren't super clean. And, as far as the servants knew, they were filled with water—and maybe nasty-smelling foot water, at that.

That being the case, pouring some of that water into a cup and asking someone to drink it was a big, big risk. The "master of the banquet" would've been a close friend or family member who took charge of the celebration, kind of like Billy Crystal hosting the Academy Awards. So if the servant said, "Hey, we found some more wine," and then the master got a mouthful of dirty water—that probably would've cut down on the servant's Christmas bonus (once such a thing was invented, of course).

Surprisingly, the servants did what Jesus asked. We don't know why they did it. They may have had some prior knowledge of Jesus and the miraculous circumstances of His birth. They may have sensed something special in the way He walked and talked—some kind of authority that made Him the kind of person you obey without question. The Bible doesn't give us a window into their motivations; it just tells us they obeyed.

Drinking a Miraculous Solution

The result was a miracle. When the master of the banquet drank, he was amazed at the quality of the wine. He even called the bridegroom over and said, in effect: "Everyone else gives people the good wine first, then breaks out the cheap stuff once people are drunk. So why have you saved the best wine for last?"

This particular miracle wasn't flashy or flamboyant. It didn't bring a lot of attention Jesus's way. But it was Jesus's first public act of supernatural power, and for those lucky enough to understand what happened, it became a miracle of an extraordinarily excellent vintage.

Key Bible Passage to Remember

"What Jesus did here in Cana of Galilee was the first of the signs through which he revealed his glory; and his disciples believed in him." (John 2:11)

Some people feel confused after reading about Jesus turning water into wine because there didn't seem to be any spiritual aspect to the act—no blind person gaining sight or dead person coming back to life. The truth is that Jesus's first miracle shows that he cares for people's needs—even something as ordinary as wine at a party. And His miracles lead to people believing in Him and making decisions to follow Him for the rest of their lives.

Lost and Found

The Prodigal Son
(Luke 15:11–32)

There are many different kinds of stories in the world today. There are long stories and short stories, bland stories and exciting stories, complicated stories and simple stories. You can find stories in any number of genres, including sci-fi, romance, adventure, horror, and many more. But there's one type of story that's largely missing from our cultural lexicon: the parable.

A parable is a short, simple story that communicates a moral lesson or truth. Parables were not meant to be historically accurate; rather, they were fictional stories told for a specific purpose. These stories were very common in the ancient world, and they were considered to be a great way to package spiritual lessons—which is why several ancient teachers, including Jesus, relied heavily on parables to train their students. In fact, several of Jesus's parables are numbered among the best-known stories in the world.

One of those well-loved stories is the parable of the Prodigal Son.

A Rebel without a Cause

Jesus's parable started with a father and two sons. The older son was industrious and hardworking—a typical firstborn child. But the second son was a rebel. He had no interest in spending the prime of his life in his father's household, only to be bossed around by his older brother once Dad passed away. So he took a step that was both bold and foolish: he demanded that his father immediately give him whatever money was part of his inheritance.

This was an extremely insulting request. The son was basically saying: "I care more about your money than I care about you, and it's not worth my time to sit around here and wait for you to die. So I want to pretend you're dead so I can get my cash and hit the road."

The father agreed to his son's demand, which would've been very surprising to Jesus's listeners because of the disrespect involved. What's not surprising is that the son didn't have a sound financial plan worked out to handle his newly acquired wealth. In fact, if you've ever paid attention to what many NFL rookies do after they sign multimillion-dollar contracts, you already know what happened next: he partied, *hard*.

The Bible says the son "squandered his wealth in wild living."[78] He bought new clothes. He wined and dined himself at fancy restaurants every night. He paid for companionship with women of ill repute to stave off the loneliness of being away from his family.

Inevitably, of course, the money ran out. Worse, it ran out right before an especially bad famine hit the land, which severely limited his prospects for employment. One week he was living large as the center of attention, loved by all. The next week he was down in the dumps—friendless, penniless, and possessing no hope for the future.

Without any other options, the son took a job feeding the pigs owned by a local farmer. And in case you're wondering, that job didn't come with health benefits and a pension plan back then. In fact, things were so bad that the son "longed to fill his stomach with the pods that the pigs were eating, but no one gave him anything."[79]

He hit rock bottom and he didn't even bounce.

An Unexpected Love

Eventually, the young son came to his senses. He realized that even the servants in his father's house ate good food every day and were compensated well for their work. So he decided to return home—but not as his father's son. He understood he'd already blown that gig. He'd basically said he wished his father was dead, which didn't leave a lot of wiggle room for sub-sequent explanations.

Therefore, the son decided to return to his father as a worker, not as his child. He would ask for a job as a servant. He even wrote up a speech as he traveled along the road: "Father, I have sinned against heaven and against you. I am no longer worthy to be called your son; make me like one of your hired servants."[80]

The text says the father saw his son "while he was still a long way off,"[81] which meant he'd been watching and waiting for his son's return. The father ran out to meet his boy, and the son started in on his speech: "Father, I have sinned against heaven and against you. I am no longer worthy to be called your son . . ."

But before the boy even finished his speech, his father gathered him up in a bear hug. He kissed him. He yelled for the servants and ordered them to find the best robe in the house and give it to the boy to wear, plus a ring for his finger—oh, and he instructed them to prepare the fatted calf and set up a party for that night.

There's a strange part at the end where the older son gets a little grumpy. He'd been working diligently in the field every day since his brother ran off, and he was displeased to see his father welcome the younger boy back home with open arms. He even refused to join in the party. "All these years I've been slaving for you and never disobeyed your orders," he said. "But when this son of yours who has squandered your property with prostitutes comes home, you kill the fattened calf for him!"[82]

The father would have none of it, however. His boy was lost, but he'd come home! That was all that mattered.

Key Bible Passage to Remember

"Bring the fattened calf and kill it. Let's have a feast and celebrate. For this son of mine was dead and is alive again; he was lost and is found." (Luke 15:23–24)

Jesus's purpose in relating this parable was to illustrate the unquenchable love God has for all His children—and the joy God experiences when people who are lost in their sin finally come to their senses and return to His love, no matter what road they travel to get there.

Won't You Be My Neighbor?

The Good Samaritan
(Luke 10:25–37)

Pop quiz! Take a moment to think about the TV shows you've watched this week, then answer this question: Did you see any examples of good neighbors in those shows?

Don't be surprised if you can't think of any right away. It's pretty slim pickings out there. Today, the best neighbor we can hope for on TV is probably Ned Flanders—he has to put up with Homer and the other Simpsons. At worst, our examples of neighborliness include all of the *Mob Wives* and any character on *Family Guy*.

That wasn't always the case. There used to be plenty of good neighbors floating around the silver screen. Think of Mister Rogers, for example, when he asks kids, "Won't you be my neighbor?" What could be a more neighborly sentiment than that from a nicer guy? Sure, there was Eddie Haskell back in the day, but for every one of him there were two neighbors like Fred and Ethel Mertz from *I Love Lucy*. Even twenty years ago we had Wilson giving great advice on *Home Improvement* and the cast of *Friends* showing everyone how to be friendly.

Still, we can take comfort in knowing we're not the only generation that's struggled to find a good definition of "neighborly" behavior. In fact, Jesus offered one of His most famous parables in order to illustrate what it truly means to be a good neighbor.

Have I Got a Story for You

It all started one day when Jesus was teaching a crowd, and an "expert in the law" (a religious leader) stood up to test Him with a question: "Teacher," he asked, "what must I do to inherit eternal life?"[83] Jesus turned the tables on the guy. He said, in effect, "What do you think the answer is?"

The expert gave a correct interpretation of the law—that we should love God with everything in us and love our neighbors as ourselves—and Jesus agreed with his words. That should've been the end of it. But the text says that the expert "wanted to justify himself," so he asked Jesus another question: "And who is my neighbor?"[84]

Instead of a straightforward answer, Jesus told

the story that we know today as the parable of the Good Samaritan.

So Many Reasons Not to Help

In the story, a man was traveling along the road connecting Jerusalem with Jericho. That was a particularly infamous stretch of road because it had a lot of twists and turns, and a lot of caves where bandits could hide and jump out to ambush travelers.

Sure enough, the traveler in Jesus's story was attacked and robbed. But the robbers weren't satisfied with just stealing his stuff; they also beat him up until he was "half dead."[85] Then they left him lying next to the road in the heat of the day.

Sometime later, a priest came down the same road. In the Jewish culture of that day, priests were a potent mix of religious authority and political power. They were God's representatives, speaking on His behalf among the people. They were well educated and usually somewhat wealthy. So if somebody was lying beaten and bleeding on the side of the road, his best hope was that the next person to come by would be a priest—the type of person most likely to help.

In Jesus's story, however, the priest didn't stop. He shuffled over to the other side of the road in order to steer clear of the beaten man, then continued on his way.

Later, another man came walking down the

road—this time a Levite. In Jesus's times, Levites served in the temple; they functioned as assistants for the priests. So a listener back then might've thought: *Well, the priests do act kind of high and mighty, but the Levites are regular people, like us. Surely he'll stop and help the injured man.*

But the Levite in Jesus's story didn't stop. He hurried on by, just as the priest did. There were a lot of great excuses available to them both—the situation is too messy, they might get mugged as well, they might miss an important appointment to help someone else. Can't get around it, though—they left a man in dire straits.

A Most Unlikely Hero

After the Levite, a Samaritan came strolling down the road. Now, you'll have to imagine Jesus's listeners shuffling their feet and scowling when they heard the word "Samaritan." That's because the Jewish people of Jesus's day considered Samaritans to be inferior and more than a little offensive. They were half Jewish and half Gentile, which meant the "real" Jewish people wanted nothing to do with them.

Imagine the audience's shock, then, when the Samaritan in Jesus's story did what the priest and the Levite failed to do: he took pity on the injured man. He stopped along the road and bandaged the man's wounds, pouring oil and wine over the bandages—a first-century form of first aid. Then the Samaritan loaded the traveler onto his donkey and took him to an inn. He cared for the man all day, and the next morning he left a bunch of money with the innkeeper and said, "Look after him . . . and when I return, I will reimburse you for any extra expense you may have."[86]

When he finished the story, Jesus turned to the "expert in the law" and asked, "Which of these three do you think was a neighbor to the man who fell into the hands of robbers?"[87] Talk about a loaded question! The expert grudgingly admitted, "The one who had mercy on him."[88] (He couldn't even bring himself to use the word "Samaritan," he was so discombobulated by Jesus's story.) Then Jesus dropped the final hammer by issuing a command to the expert, to the crowd, and to every person who hears His parable today: "Go and do likewise."[89]

Through this masterful story, Jesus made it clear that a neighbor is anyone who needs our help, no matter how offensive the person or how inconvenient the situation—and that we have a responsibility to treat our neighbors in the same way that we would like to be treated ourselves.

Key Bible Passage to Remember

"He answered, 'Love the Lord your God with all your heart and with all your soul and with all your strength and with all your mind,' and, 'Love your neighbor as yourself.'" (Luke 10:27)

Spoken by the "expert in the law" and confirmed by Jesus, these words are an excellent summary of what the Bible has to say about living as a member of God's kingdom here on earth.

Master of the Wind and Waves

Jesus Walks on Water
(Matthew 14:22–36 and Mark 4:35–41)

Everyone has to go through bad weather from time to time. These experiences are usually mild, and they vary by location—thunderstorms in one region of the world, blizzards in another, and dust storms in another still. But some storms are severe, even life-changing. Hurricanes are an example, as are tornadoes, monsoons, haboobs (severe sandstorms), tsunamis, and more. Those are the storms we typically remember as the years go by.

It's appropriate, then, that Jesus's disciples had one of their most memorable and life-changing encounters with Him in the middle of a particularly violent storm.

Shortcut to the Boat

Jesus was teaching along the Sea of Galilee, which is really a freshwater lake located on the northeast border of modern Israel. As He was dismissing the crowds one evening, Jesus decided to teach in another village the next day, so He instructed His disciples to get in their boat and row across to the other side of the sea.

Jesus didn't go with them, however. He stayed behind to finish dispersing the crowd, and then He went up into the mountainous area next to the sea to pray. Jesus stayed in the mountains for several hours, until the countryside had become fully dark.

Meanwhile, Jesus's disciples were experiencing some trouble. They'd been caught in a squall that came down over the mountains and flashed across the sea—a common phenomenon in that region. Many of the disciples were experienced fishermen, which meant they were used to those kinds of storms. Even so, the Gospel of Mark says the boat "was in the middle of the lake"[90] when Jesus came down from the mountains and spotted them. That means the disciples had been rowing for several hours without making much progress against the wind and the waves.

Here's what happened next, according to the text: "Shortly before dawn Jesus went out to them, walking on the lake."[91] Jesus wanted to meet His disciples on the other side of the sea, so He decided to take a little stroll. On foot. Over the water. In the middle of a storm so violent even experienced fishermen with a boat and oars and sails were having trouble making any progress.

It was one of Jesus's most surprising miracles, and the disciples were certainly shocked, even a bit terrified, when they saw Him coming. Understandably, they had a hard time recognizing Jesus in the middle of the storm, and so they thought they were seeing a ghost. All of them were so distracted they forgot about rowing and cried out in fear.

The World's Best Lifeguard

Jesus heard their cries, of course, and He made His way over to the boat. He said: "Take courage! It is I. Don't be afraid."[92] And that's when things got *really* interesting.

Peter was an especially outgoing disciple of Jesus. He was fiercely loyal and incredibly foolish at the same time. He had a big heart and an even bigger mouth. To put it another way, Peter was a character—think of a combination of Kenneth Parcell from *30 Rock* and Cosmo Kramer from *Seinfeld*. (Well, maybe that's an exaggeration.) Anyway, when Peter heard Jesus speaking from the middle of the storm, he had a crazy idea. "Lord, if it's you," Peter said, "tell me to come to you on the water."[93]

Now, we don't know what motivations Peter had for making such a request. The Bible doesn't tell us what was going through his mind. We only know that he wanted to imitate this stupendous feat—and that Jesus, incredibly, said, "Come."[94]

So Peter came. He hopped out of the boat and, just as Jesus had, landed solidly on top of the water. Imagine how exhilarated Peter must have felt as he lifted up one foot, then the other, and the weight of gravity didn't affect him as he walked on the water toward Jesus. What a rush!

Unfortunately for Peter, it didn't last very long. As he continued walking away from the other disciples, he began to realize what was happening around him. He heard the sounds of the wind whipping at his clothes. He saw the waves rolling around him and crashing violently into the boat. He felt the spray of the water splash across his face and arms. As he came to his senses, so to speak, his fear of the storm trumped his trust in Jesus—and immediately he sank into the sea.

Fortunately for Peter, Jesus is the best lifeguard anyone could ever ask for, and He quickly grabbed hold of His sinking friend and hauled him out of the water. As they made their way back to the boat, Jesus both chastised and encouraged Peter by saying: "You of little faith . . . why did you doubt?"[95]

What He Did for an Encore

That wasn't Jesus's only nautical miracle. Storms at sea just didn't faze Him. Another time, He was catching a nap in the stern of a boat as another storm blew furiously about him and the disciples. The disciples mistook this behavior for indifference and, waking Him, said, "Teacher, don't you care if we drown?" Jesus rebuked the wind and said to the waves, "Quiet! Be still!"[96] The sea became as flat as a pancake and no air stirred. Once again, Jesus questioned why the disciples' growing faith, which had been nourished by watching Him perform miracles, suddenly withered away into doubt and fear. Ultimately, though, the disciples' wonder and awe overcame their sense of shame at not comprehending Jesus's unlimited power.

Something interesting happened in the minds and hearts of the disciples after Jesus performed these two miracles. After everything they'd heard about Jesus and everything they'd seen Him accomplish, this was the moment when the lights came on and they actually *understood* the full implications of what they'd witnessed. Although they at first questioned what they saw—who in the world could have the forces of nature obey his voice and hand signals?—they could only conclude that this flesh-and-blood man standing in the boat was actually the all-powerful and only God, in the flesh. In other words, it wasn't until the disciples experienced Jesus's faithfulness in the middle of the storm that they truly grasped His divine power and love, and they believed.

Key Bible Passage to Remember

"But when he saw the wind, he was afraid and, beginning to sink, cried out, 'Lord, save me!'" (Matthew 14:30)

Peter often catches a lot of flak when people tell this story. They concentrate on his lack of faith and the indignity of failing in front of Jesus. But the truth is we all fail. We all lack faith at times, and so we all need to remember—as Peter did—that Jesus is our only hope for salvation.

The Three Superheroes

Moses, Elijah, and Jesus Transformed
(Matthew 17:1–21; Luke 9:28–43)

Sometimes it feels like you can't throw a rock these days without hitting a new superhero movie. It all started when Marvel's *X-Men* grossed more than $150 million at the box office back in 2000. Since then, we've seen a steady stream of spandex-wearing, villain-defeating heroes saving the world over and over again on the big screen. There's *Spider Man, Iron Man, The Dark Knight, The Green Lantern*. And a host of them together in *The Avengers*.

Why are these movies (and the comic books that preceded them) so popular? Why are people willing to watch the same situations play out again and again, often with largely the same results? We love the scenarios of others who are more than human—superhuman, if you will—fighting for our good against enormous, superhuman odds.

This isn't a modern phenomenon, either. Even

Jesus's disciples had heroes from the past who were involved in amazing feats, and the Bible includes a story in which three of the disciples got to meet a couple of those heroes face-to-face.

A Mountaintop Experience

Jesus kept a rigorous pace during His time in ancient Israel. He traveled from village to village, teaching about His heavenly Father and Himself as the fulfillment of the Scriptures, and performing many signs and wonders for people in need. But the Bible also records several occasions when Jesus intentionally left the crowds behind in order to pray and recharge. Sometimes He was alone on these retreats, and sometimes He brought the disciples with Him.

The latter was the case when Jesus hiked up an isolated mountain in the region of Nazareth—but He didn't bring all the disciples, just His three most trusted companions: Peter, James, and John. Those three men didn't realize it as they laboriously followed Jesus around rocks and up steep inclines, but they were going to have one of the most incredible experiences of their lives. What they were about to witness is commonly known as the Transfiguration.

At the top of the mountain, Jesus led the three men in an extended period of prayer and meditation. After such a long hike, however, Peter, James, and John weren't feeling super spiritual. In fact, the text says, "Peter and his companions were very sleepy."[97] They dozed off. And when they woke up, their entire world was changed.

When they opened their eyes, they saw Jesus—but it wasn't the Jesus they were familiar with. It was Jesus transformed. "His face shone like the sun," according to the Gospel of Matthew, "and his clothes became as white as the light."[98] Luke wrote that "the appearance of his face changed, and his clothes became as bright as a flash of lightning."[99] In other words, Jesus no longer looked like a normal human being. He shone supernaturally, with divine glory.

But that wasn't the craziest part of the whole experience for the disciples. What really shook them up was that Jesus had been joined by two other people—Moses and Elijah. (You can read more details about both men in other stories in this volume.)

It's important to understand that Moses and Elijah were absolutely revered by the Jews of Jesus's day. They'd been central spiritual leaders from Israel's ancient past. They'd single-handedly saved the nation at various times from the gravest dangers, both political and moral.

So if we could wrap George Washington, Billy Graham, and Martin Luther King, Jr., into a single person—that would be similar to what Peter, James, and John saw when they looked at Moses and Elijah standing in front of them, just shooting the breeze with Jesus.

Needless to say, Jesus's disciples were flummoxed. James and John were speechless, while Peter, with his usual hubris, blurted out, "Master, it is good for us to be here. Let us put up three shelters—one for you, one for Moses and one for Elijah."[100] Peter wanted to camp out and have a long chat with the men he'd heard stories about his whole life. He didn't understand that something bigger was happening, but he found out fairly quickly.

Before Jesus could respond to Peter's suggestion, a cloud enveloped the mountain. Then a voice spoke out of the cloud, saying: "This is my Son, whom I have chosen; listen to him."[101] It was the voice of God the Father, and it made the disciples feel afraid. This was getting way beyond their comfort zone. It also showed them what they should have recognized all along—that as important as Moses and Elijah may have been in terms of their past, Jesus was the true Hero in their midst and the hope of their future. They needed to pay a lot more attention to the One who mattered most. Suddenly the vision was over and only Jesus, in normal human appearance, remained.

Champion of the (Spiritual) World

Peter, James, and John were reminded yet again of Jesus's true identity on the following morning, when they followed Him down the mountain. A crowd was already waiting at the bottom, anxious to hear more from Jesus and to see what He might do.

A man in the crowd cried out to Jesus, saying, "Teacher, I beg you to look at my son, for he is my only child."[102] Jesus came to him. The man explained that his son was possessed by a demon, which sent the boy into convulsions and caused him to foam at the mouth. The boy was dying, and the man had begged Jesus's other disciples to get rid of the demon—but they were unable to.

Even as his father spoke, the boy was thrown to the ground and began to shake violently. Jesus immediately rebuked the demon, and the boy was healed. Just like that. Appropriately, the text says the people in the crowd "were all amazed at the greatness of God."[103] He had authority over all spiritual forces in the universe.

Peter, James, and John were also amazed, but for them Jesus's actions were another reminder of what they'd seen and heard on the mountain. Moses and Elijah had been great men who forever changed the nation of Israel. But Jesus was more than a man, and He'd come on a mission to forever change the world.

Key Bible Passage to Remember

"While he was still speaking, a bright cloud covered them, and a voice from the cloud said, 'This is my Son, whom I love; with him I am well pleased. Listen to him!'" (Matthew 17:5)

One of the key tenets of the Christian faith is that Jesus Christ was both fully human and fully divine. He was a man, just as Moses and Elijah were. And yet Jesus's Being also incorporated infinitely more than Moses, Elijah, or any of us will ever experience. He was a man who possessed the full power and authority of God Himself.

The Man Who Died Twice

The Raising of Lazarus
(John 11:1–44)

Steve Jobs passed away on October 5, 2011. He was a cultural icon in many ways and an inspiration to many people. Yet ironically, one of the things that helped propel Jobs to achieve great things in the world was the knowledge that he would one day leave it. "Remembering that I'll be dead soon is the most important tool I've ever encountered to help me make the big choices in life," he said. "Because almost everything—all external expectations, all pride, all fear of embarrassment or failure—these things just fall away in the face of death, leaving only what is truly important."[104]

Like Steve Jobs, a man named Lazarus understood how the inevitability of death can influence our decisions in life. Unlike Steve Jobs, however,

Lazarus didn't come to those conclusions until *after* he died.

Waking the Dead

Because Jesus and His disciples traveled among so many different towns and villages on their teaching circuit, they often depended on the hospitality of their supporters for shelter and food. In the town of Bethany, one of Jesus's main supporters was a man named Lazarus. We don't know much about this man—only that he had two sisters, Mary and Martha, and that Jesus and His disciples stopped by Lazarus's house on a number of occasions.[105]

One day Jesus was teaching in another village when He received word that Lazarus was very sick. Lazarus's sisters, Mary and Martha, had sent a messenger to give Jesus the news and request that He come to Bethany and heal their brother as quickly as possible.

Now, on the one hand, it was certainly bold of the sisters to request that Jesus drop everything and come to their brother's aid. This was Jesus, after all! He had kind of a busy schedule. On the other hand, the text says: "Jesus loved Martha and her sister and Lazarus."[106] So the sisters felt Jesus would want to come, given His affection for them and their brother.

But Jesus didn't come—at least not right away. He stayed where He was for another two days before

He finally gathered His disciples together and told them He wanted to travel to Bethany. "Our friend Lazarus has fallen asleep," He told them, "but I am going there to wake him up."[107]

Jesus Wept

By the time Jesus and His disciples reached Bethany, they found a somber scene. Lazarus was dead, and he'd already been buried and sealed in a tomb within one of the many caves dotting the landscape of that region. It was over. End of story.

Almost as soon as He arrived, Jesus was confronted by Martha, Lazarus's sister. She knew that Jesus had delayed traveling to Bethany, and she was blunt in her assessment of His decision: "Lord," she said, "if you had been here, my brother would not have died."[108]

Jesus's answer was strange, terrifying, and exciting all at the same time. He said, "Your brother will rise again."[109]

Martha went home and told her sister that Jesus had arrived, and Mary quickly came out to greet Him. Her message was the same as her sister's had been: "Lord, if you had been here, my brother would not have died."[110] Seeing her pain and the sorrow of Lazarus's friends, many of whom had come from Jerusalem to pay their respects, Jesus was deeply moved. He grieved with them, even to the point of weeping openly.

Many in the crowd were impressed by Jesus's tears because they understood that He truly loved Lazarus. But others whispered behind His back, saying, "Could not he who opened the eyes of the blind man have kept this man from dying?"[111] Fortunately for Lazarus, the answer to that question was yes.

It Ain't Over 'Til It's Over

Jesus asked the sisters to show Him Lazarus's tomb, which was normal—people visited grave sites back then, just as we do today. But then Jesus asked Martha to open the tomb, which was most definitely *not* normal. The tomb had been sealed, and Martha quickly informed Jesus of what everyone else considered obvious. "Lord," she said, "by this time there is a bad odor, for he has been there four days."[112] (Martha was the practical sister, in case you hadn't noticed.)

Jesus told Martha not to be afraid, but to believe—and that in doing so she would see the glory of God. So Martha gave the signal, and several of the onlookers removed the stone that had sealed Lazarus's tomb. Then Jesus prayed, thanking the Father for hearing His words and helping those who were watching to believe.

Then, in a loud voice filled with divine authority, Jesus said: "Lazarus, come out!"[113] And to the utter astonishment of everyone watching, Lazarus obeyed

Jesus's voice. He was still wrapped in the shroud in which he'd been buried, but Lazarus came walking out on his own two feet. He had a new lease on life, and, as Yogi Berra once said of baseball: "It ain't over 'til it's over." And even though Lazarus would have to die later, a second time, it wouldn't be over even then, according to Jesus. Another—eternal—life awaited beyond.

By demonstrating power over life and death, Jesus opened the door for the possibility of His own resurrection. And that meant that, in the long run, death could be, and would be, swallowed up by life— eternal life for all who believe in Him.

Key Bible Passage to Remember

"Jesus said to her, 'I am the resurrection and the life. The one who believes in me will live, even though they die; and whoever lives by believing in me will never die.'" (*John* 11:25–26)

Lazarus's release from the tomb was a remarkable event, but it was also a miracle of limited scope. That's because Lazarus eventually died again, and that time he stayed dead, as the rest of us do. What's most valuable about Lazarus's story, however, is that it foreshadows the victorious resurrection of Jesus Christ, who burst forth from the grave—and never returned, as Lazarus later did—after securing salvation for all people.

A Meal to Remember

The Last Supper
(Matthew 26:17–35; Luke 22:7–38; John 13:1–38)

One of the undeniable advantages of living in the United States during this specific moment in history is that most people are never very far away from a good meal. If you're willing to hop in a car, you can find the type of cuisine you're looking for—Mexican, Thai, Italian, Himalayan, Indian, barbecue, Mediterranean, kosher, and more. And if all else fails, you can swing by the supermarket and pick up ingredients for whatever you're willing (and able) to cook.

They didn't have so many food choices back in ancient Israel, but that didn't stop Jesus from presiding over one of the most influential meals in history—one that's still commemorated by millions of modern Christians each and every week through the practice of what is known as Holy Communion, the Eucharist, or the Lord's Supper.

Kosher All the Way

For thousands of years, Jewish communities have observed the Feast of Unleavened Bread in order to remember and celebrate the Israelites' freedom from slavery in Egypt. Also known as Passover, the feast is seven days long and begins with a special meal called the seder, which commemorates the evening on which the angel of the Lord struck down the first-born children of the Egyptians but "passed over" the children of the Israelites. (See "Let My People Go!" on page 32.)

Because Jesus and all His disciples were Jewish, they traveled to Jerusalem every year to celebrate the Passover. This was a regular custom among the Jews—anyone who lived away from the temple would make an effort to travel to Jerusalem in order to celebrate the major religious feasts, including Passover.

One year, on the first day of Passover—in the last week of Jesus's life—the disciples were worried about where they would eat the seder meal. So Jesus gave them a set of instructions: "Go into the city to a certain man and tell him, 'The Teacher says: My appointed time is near. I am going to celebrate the Passover with my disciples at your house.'"[114]

The disciples didn't know what Jesus meant by "My appointed time is near," but they did understand that they were going to get free food and drink. They were happy to do what Jesus asked.

The Servant Leader

The seder meal started out normally enough. Everyone reclined around the low table, lying on their sides and propping themselves on one elbow—that was the custom in those days. But after only a few minutes, Jesus started to say and do several things that the disciples found most difficult to swallow.

First, Jesus blessed the cup of wine and instructed the disciples to divide it among themselves, which was traditional. But then He told them He wouldn't drink the fruit of the vine again until the coming of God's kingdom. The disciples had no idea what He was talking about. Then Jesus divided up the unleavened bread and said, "This is my body given for you."[115] Huh? Then Jesus poured out more wine and said, "This cup is the new covenant in my blood, which is poured out for you."[116] Double huh?

Then things really got crazy. Jesus got up, walked away from the table, and started taking His clothes off. He stripped off His outer garments and wrapped a cloth around His waist. Then He picked up a basin of water and began to wash the disciples' feet.

Now, that probably sounds strange to you, but it was downright shocking for the disciples. Jerusalem was a sandy, dusty city in those days, and most people wore sandals when they walked around—which meant people's feet were always filthy by the end of the day. That's why wealthy individuals gave their lowest-ranking servants the job of filling a bucket of water and washing off the stinky, grime-encrusted feet of their guests before the evening meal.

So this means Jesus was doing something that even Mike Rowe would be embarrassed to do on *Dirty Jobs*. That's why Peter, the loudmouthed disciple, didn't want anything to do with whatever Jesus had in mind. He said, "[Y]ou shall never wash my feet." But Jesus answered him by saying, "Unless I wash you, you have no part with me."[117] So Peter overcompensated and asked that Jesus wash his whole body, which was not the intention. Jesus said He was only wanting to perform a symbolic act that had a deeper spiritual meaning, not give Peter a full bath.

When He finished washing, Jesus taught them a crucial lesson. He reminded them that He was the Master in the room, and they were His followers. And if He was willing to humble Himself in order to serve His followers, they should be more than willing to let go of their pride and serve one another—not to mention serve the world.

Betrayal, Sorrow, Despair

Before leaving their accommodations, Jesus delivered two pieces of news—both of them bad.

First, he announced that one of His disciples would betray Him. He even identified that disciple as Judas Iscariot by handing him a piece of bread and saying, "What you are about to do, do quickly."[118] Judas—a charlatan and a thief, who as a money-keeper had helped himself to the charitable contributions for their ministry—rushed out of the room and went straight to the Pharisees and other religious leaders who wanted Jesus dead because He'd claimed to be God. Later in the evening, Judas helped that group arrest Jesus, which eventually led to His crucifixion. (If you remember Cypher from *The Matrix*, you've got the right idea.)

Second, Jesus told Peter that he would deny Him three times before the next morning—a serious breach of loyalty. Peter argued with Jesus up and down; he claimed he was willing to die for his Master no matter what happened. But he was wrong. After Jesus was arrested, Peter pretended three times not to know Jesus in order to avoid being arrested, too. When he realized what he'd done, the text says he "wept bitterly."[119] In other words, he repented of his betrayal; whereas Judas, realizing the enormity of his crime against an innocent man, put a noose around his own neck and hanged himself from the nearest tree. One man found forgiveness, the other only despair. Peter got the message and, in his new-found humility, went on to be the servant-leader Jesus envisioned.

Key Bible Passage to Remember

"In the same way, after the supper he took the cup, saying, 'This cup is the new covenant in my blood, which is poured out for you.'" (Luke 22:20)

Jesus intended the Last Supper to be a symbolic reminder for all people of our need for a new way to escape the mess of the world—a "new covenant." And because He was willing to shed His blood on our behalf, we are able to break free and experience the saving power of that covenant both now and forevermore.

The Cross That Rocked the World

The Crucifixion
(Matthew 27:11–56; Luke 23:26–49;
John 19:17–37)

Every generation is marked by specific days so important they stand out from all the rest—moments in history that ring out beyond their normal time and send shock waves reverberating through cultures. Think of November 22, 1963, for example, which is the day John F. Kennedy was assassinated. Or November 9, 1989, when the Berlin Wall finally fell. And, of course, there is September 11, 2001.

We don't know the exact date of Jesus's death in ancient Jerusalem. But we do know the crucifixion was the most influential historical event the world has ever seen. And we know the impact of that event is still changing lives and changing the world thousands of years later.

Forgive Their Torture and Humiliation

After being betrayed by one of His disciples and arrested by the religious leaders in Jerusalem, Jesus was run through a series of sham trials throughout the night and into the morning. Shuffling Him between different groups of religious and political authorities, the Pharisees claimed that Jesus was rebelling against Caesar, since He'd spoken about establishing God's kingdom on earth.

During the trials, Jesus was slapped, beaten, and whipped cruelly across His back with a torture device called a cat-o'-nine-tails. Roman soldiers twisted together a crown made out of thorns and jammed it onto His head. Then they draped Him in a purple robe, spit on Him, and mock-saluted Him as the new "so-called" king of the Jews. Eventually the Roman governor of Jerusalem, Pontius Pilate, sentenced Jesus to be killed by crucifixion—a terrible death usually reserved for only the worst traitors and rebels against the Empire.

The local authorities didn't waste any time in carrying out the sentence. Soldiers grabbed a rough-hewn chunk of wood about six feet long—part of Jesus's cross—and forced him to carry it through the streets of Jerusalem along with two other prisoners who were also scheduled to be crucified. When Jesus was unable to go any farther because of the wounds He'd received, the soldiers forced a man named

Simon to join the procession behind Jesus and carry His cross to its destination.

The procession left the city and made its way to an area called Golgotha, also known as the Skull[120] because a rocky crag overlooking the street resembled a human skull (and still does). There, the soldiers tied Jesus's arms to the chunk of wood, then nailed Him in place using long iron spikes. Then they used the wood to lift Jesus off His feet so that He was hanging by the spikes in his wrists. The soldiers pinned Jesus's feet to the bottom of the vertical beam and used more spikes to nail them in place.

When they finished, Jesus looked up toward heaven and said, "Father, forgive them, for they do not know what they are doing."[121] A very unusual response under the circumstances, but then again, they actually didn't know what was happening in the grander scheme of things.

Quick Trip to Heaven

One of the reasons crucifixion was such a horrible way to die is that the Romans designed it to take as long as possible. Victims were nailed to a cross with their legs bent at the knees, which meant that the weight of their torsos pulled against the nails driven through their wrists. In order to breathe properly, victims had to push upward with their legs, which placed tremendous pressure on the nails driven through their feet.

Yet even with all the pain involved, it was common for people to remain alive for two or three days while hanging from their crosses.

Another reason crucifixion was so terrible is that it was extremely humiliating. Victims were hung on their crosses without any clothes. And the crosses themselves were arranged on the side of busy roads, so that as many people as possible would see what would happen to someone who defied the Roman Empire.

The Bible records several people interacting with Jesus while He hung from the cross. Most mocked Him. They said, "Come down from the cross, if you are the Son of God!"[122] And, "He saved others . . . but he can't save himself!"[123] Others spit on Him and shouted insults at Him as they walked along the road.

Perversely, one of the criminals crucified next to Jesus also threw insults at Him. But the second criminal understood the gravity of what was happening. "Don't you fear God?" he asked the first, "since you are under the same sentence? We are punished justly, for we are getting what our deeds deserve. But this man has done nothing wrong."[124]

Then the second criminal said, "Jesus, remember me when you come into your kingdom."[125] Jesus answered, "Truly I tell you, today you will be with me in paradise."[126] Even as His life slowly and painfully slipped away, Jesus was focused on saving others.

Not a Happy Ending ... Yet

At about noon, the sky began to grow dark over Jerusalem. The darkness lasted for three hours, until the people watching the crucifixion could hardly see. Then Jesus cried out in a loud voice, "My God, my God, why have you forsaken me?"[127] He was quoting the first line of a poem (Psalm 22) written by His ancestor King David. But near the end of that same poem is an upbeat note in verse 24: "[H]e [God the Father] has not hidden his face from him, but has listened to his cry for help."

Jesus cried out again and then, more softly, He said, "It is finished." Exhaling one last time, He "bowed his head and gave up his spirit."[128] It was over.

But many of the people watching didn't notice Jesus's death because, at that moment, a tremendous earthquake shook the ground around them. It was as if the very rocks understood that something both momentous and unthinkable had happened, even if the onlookers had no idea.

The Pharisees didn't want the executions to drag into Saturday, the Sabbath, so they asked the Roman soldiers to break the legs of each man, thus cutting off their ability to breathe. The soldiers didn't strike Jesus's legs, however. They didn't need to. He was dead. The true Light of the world had, for a time, been extinguished.

Key Bible Passage to Remember

"And when Jesus had cried out again in a loud voice, he gave up his spirit. At that moment the curtain of the temple was torn in two from top to bottom." *(Matthew 27:50–51)*

The "curtain of the temple" was a thick piece of material that barred entrance to a room called the Holy of Holies, where the presence of God dwelt in the temple of Jerusalem. For thousands of years, people had been forbidden from passing through that curtain—forbidden from encountering God directly. But Jesus's sacrifice changed everything; it gave all people the opportunity to approach God as His children and to experience His presence.

SonRise in Jerusalem

The Easter Story
(Matthew 28:1–20; Luke 24:1–49)

"Almost dead" scenes are a favorite trick of Hollywood screenwriters and directors. That's when a major character—usually the hero or the hero's love interest—gets badly injured near the end of a movie, and we're led to believe that character might be dead.

What happens to Neo at the end of the first *Matrix* movie is a pretty good example of an "almost dead" scene. Keanu Reeves gets shot in the chest multiple times, and the monitor plugged into his mind devolves into a sinister, monotone hum. Mournful music starts playing in the background as other characters lean over him and say, "It can't be." But then Neo's love interest starts talking about how he can't be dead because she's just started to believe, and she kisses him for the first time, and then—boom! Neo's back up and using mind-control powers to kill the bad guys.

Good stuff, right? There are hundreds of similar scenes in popular movies. And the reason filmmakers keep replicating the same basic idea is because we as movie watchers love last-minute surprises and happy endings. We love the idea that there's still a chance—that death might not be permanent, as it is in real life.

That's just one of the reasons why the Easter story has provided hope and inspiration to millions of people over the past two thousand years.

The Spice Girls Encounter Jesus

To be fair, the difference between "almost dead" scenes and the resurrection of Jesus Christ is that Jesus actually died. His heart stopped beating, His brain shut down, and His spirit departed this world. This happened on a Friday afternoon, and Jesus was buried in a tomb. He stayed in that tomb through Friday night. He stayed in that tomb all day Saturday.

Then came Sunday—the day after Passover, the first day of the week, and the day that would become the Christian Sabbath, or holy day, because of this momentous event.

At dawn, a group of brave women assembled and walked to Jesus's tomb. They carried burial spices and strips of cloth, intending to anoint Jesus's body in the proper way. They expected to have a hard time reaching His body because a huge stone had been rolled into a groove in front the tomb, sealing it shut. Also, the religious leaders had arranged for Roman guards to stand watch over the burial site because they feared that Jesus's disciples would try to steal His body. Even so, the women's love and desire to honor Jesus in burial outweighed their fears.

So they faced obstacles to their plans—the soldiers on guard, the stone firmly in place. But before the women had a chance to approach, a violent earthquake shook the ground. And then, out of nowhere, an angel nonchalantly appeared next to the tomb! The text says the angel's "appearance was like lightning"[129] and that the guards "were so afraid of him that they shook and became like dead men."[130] This was not included in their job description.

The angel walked over to the stone and rolled it away from the mouth of the tomb as easily as if it were made of Styrofoam. Ignoring the soldiers, the angel turned his attention to the women and told them not to be afraid. He said Jesus was no longer in the tomb—that He'd risen from the dead, just as He had promised. And he urged the women to see the empty grave for themselves, then hurry back to Jerusalem and tell the disciples what had happened.

The women did as they were told, and the text says they were "afraid yet filled with joy."[131] Imagine their joy, then, when they met Jesus on their way back to the city! He greeted them warmly. Just as the angel did, He told them not to be afraid, and to return quickly to the other disciples and tell them what had happened. He had great plans for all of them.

The women did return, and they spoke excitedly about all they'd seen and heard. But the men were not buying it. Most thought the women were just overexcited by recent events. Only Peter—loyal, foolish, foot-in-mouth Peter—allowed himself to hope. Without speaking to anyone, Peter jumped up and hurried to the gravesite, and likewise, John followed.

When they arrived at the tomb, Peter rushed inside and found no sign of Jesus's body—only the linen shroud in which He had been buried. John poked his head in as well and confirmed what both Peter and the women had found: Jesus was gone.

Appearances Are Not Deceiving

Later that day, two of Jesus's disciples had left Jerusalem and were walking toward the village of Emmaus. All of a sudden, out of nowhere, Jesus came strolling alongside them and struck up a conversation. These disciples thought he was a visitor from Jerusalem. The text says "they were kept from recognizing him."[132] When Jesus inquired about the major events that had taken place in recent days, the disciples told Him all about it—including what the women had seen and heard that morning.

Then Jesus began to unravel the mystery behind

the events. As they walked, He taught them all the ways the Old Testament pointed to Him and what He'd had to endure on the cross. He helped them understand God's plan to redeem humanity, and His words enabled them to understand why a sinless sacrifice was required in order to forever cleanse the continually sinful state of human beings.

When the two disciples arrived at their destination, they invited Jesus to join them for a meal, during which He revealed Himself to them. Then later, in Jerusalem, when the rest of the disciples had gathered together, Jesus appeared once again. At first the disciples thought they were seeing a ghost, but Jesus told them not to be afraid. He showed them the places in His wrists and feet where the nails had been pounded through flesh and bone. He showed them the hole in His side, where the spear had pierced Him. He even ate a piece of fish, just to show that even His digestive system was back in working order.

After all the commotion, Jesus again explained God's plan to the disciples. He told them about the true nature of the Messiah, and of the difficult road that stood before any person who followed Him. And finally the whole thing clicked for the disciples. They got it. They put their faith in Him and were willing to obey Him as their Lord. He was not a political Messiah setting up an earthly government, as they had hoped. But His resurrection from the dead became the heart of the message that the followers of Jesus spread to the ends of the earth, the very rationale for claiming Him to be the Savior of not just the Jewish nation but the entire world.

Key Bible Passage to Remember

"In their fright the women bowed down with their faces to the ground, but the men said to them, 'Why do you look for the living among the dead? He is not here; he has risen!'" (Luke 24:5–6)

No one questions that death is a powerful and tragic force within our world. But one of the most wonderful implications of Jesus's story is that death is not all-powerful—that death has actually been defeated once and for all.

Not as Drunk as You Suppose

The Apostles and Pentecost (Acts 2:1–47)

In the world of business today, companies are continually working to entice and excite a group of people known as "early adopters." These are the men and women who take particular pleasure in being among the first to try something new. Early adopters often sign up as beta testers for new products. They like to attend the grand openings of new restaurants, and they really enjoy being the first among their friends to purchase that fancy new gizmo everyone's talking about.

Evidently there were early adopters in the ancient world as well, because the book of Acts, chapter 2, describes the first people to become part of what we know today as the Christian Church.

The Answer Is Blowin' in the Wind

After Jesus's resurrection and ascension into heaven, His disciples gathered together and shut themselves in a room for several days. They spent their time worshipping and praying, as well as working out a few organizational matters—such as selecting a new disciple to replace Judas, who'd committed suicide after betraying Jesus.

But what the disciples were doing most within the confines of that room was waiting. Specifically, they were waiting for the fulfillment of the words Jesus had spoken before His ascension into heaven: "Stay in the city until you have been clothed with power from on high."[133]

The disciples didn't understand exactly what that meant, but they knew they were supposed to wait until God did something really big—something that would propel them forcefully into a new world of ministry opportunities.

It happened on the day of Pentecost, which is also a feast day for the Jewish people (who now call it Shavuot). On that day, they celebrate the harvest of the first of the new crops. The people in ancient Israel didn't yet realize they would be bringing in a first crop of new believers in Jesus. But on that particular Pentecost, the disciples suddenly heard a sound like a great rushing of wind. The sound swelled in volume, filling the room and drowning out all other noise. Then what the Bible describes as "tongues of fire"[134] appeared above each of the disciples' heads. These "tongues" were visible representations of God's glory, and were symbolic of the burning bush Moses encountered in the desert and the pillar of fire God used to lead the Israelites out of Egypt. In other words, they were evidence that God was up to something.

While all this was happening, many people in Jerusalem heard the rushing sound and gathered around the disciples' dwelling in order to see what was causing such a commotion. Soon afterward, the disciples came out of the room where they had been praying. They were filled with the Spirit of God, and they began to proclaim to the people all that God had done for them.

Now You're Speaking My Language!

At first the large crowd of onlookers thought that the disciples' words were gibberish or drunken speech, kind of like what we remember from our story of the Tower of Babel. Peter replied that he and the disciples couldn't be drunk—it was only nine o'clock in the morning! And here's the strange part: the people suddenly understood what the disciples were saying. The reason that's strange is because the city contained many thousands of Jews who'd traveled from other countries in order to celebrate the feast of Pentecost in Jerusalem. These Jews did not speak the disciples' language. They'd come from Egypt and various other parts of Africa, from Greece, from Mesopotamia and elsewhere in Asia, and beyond.

The text says the people in the streets were "utterly amazed," and they asked: "Aren't all these who are speaking Galileans? Then how is it that each of us hears them in our native language?"[135] Nobody realized it, but they were witnessing one of the greatest miracles of all time. When God poured out His spirit on the disciples, He gave them the ability to speak in languages they'd never been exposed to before, and gave each recipient the ability to hear them in his or her own language. This allowed the disciples to spread the good news of Jesus's resurrection and accompanying eternal life to everyone who heard them.

Birth of a Preacher

In the middle of all that chaos, Peter stood up to speak. Peter—the same guy who walked on the water and almost fell in, who didn't want to have his feet washed by his Master, and who recently denied he even knew Jesus at all. Seeing him, some of the other disciples may have been tempted to groan or slap a face-palm—no, not Peter. We can't afford to blow this one!

But this was not the same Peter who'd lost faith, overreacted, and lost his nerve. This was a Peter transformed by the power of God. And when he spoke, he captivated the crowd with poignant and powerful words. He explained what the disciples had experienced in the prayer room, and that it was the fulfillment of a prophecy recorded in the Old Testament.[136]

Then Peter began to speak about Jesus. He explained who Jesus was and why He'd come. He talked about Jesus's death—even reminding the people that they, "with the help of wicked men, put him to death by nailing him to the cross."[137] But God wasn't going to hold that against them! Then Peter told them how Jesus had risen from the grave, and what that meant. He told them Jesus was the Messiah that the Jews had longed for and that the entire world needed.

How May We Be of Service?

The people in the crowd were stunned. The text says "they were cut to the heart." They asked Peter and the other disciples, "Brothers, what shall we do?"[138]

So Peter told them what to do: repent of sin and turn away from it. Be baptized. Receive the gift of God's Spirit, which is now offered to all people because of what Jesus did. Christians have preached that same message for thousands of years, and Christians still preach that Good News today.

Key Bible Passage to Remember

"Every day they continued to meet together in the temple courts. They broke bread in their homes and ate together with glad and sincere hearts, praising God and enjoying the favor of all the people. And the Lord added to their number daily those who were being saved." (Acts 2:46–47)

About three thousand men and women became Christians on that day of Pentecost, which was quite an increase in church attendance, given that only around one hundred people had gathered in the disciples' room! But the multiplication didn't stop there. Those three thousand souls eventually became tens of thousands, then hundreds of thousands, then millions—and now billions, as the Church continues to grow in love and service of others even to this day.

A Most Unlikely Conversion

Paul on the Damascus Road
(Acts 9:1–31)

Religious persecution is a very real threat in today's world. Many Christians and non-Christians in a number of different countries are regularly repressed, beaten, and denied basic rights—all because of their refusal to compromise their faith. This should not be, and yet fanatical intolerance of others' spiritual beliefs has persisted for thousands of years.

The earliest Christians were often oppressed because of their beliefs, both by the Roman Empire and the Jewish religious establishment. Interestingly, the man who was most vicious in his persecution of Christians—Saul of Tarsus—became the most prolific author in the New Testament after a life-changing encounter with Jesus Christ.

Blinded by the Light

The conversion of more than three thousand Jewish men and women to Christianity on Pentecost—a major Jewish holiday, no less—did not go unnoticed by the Jewish religious leaders. Many of them were unsure of what to do. Many others were willing to have extended conversations with the followers of Jesus and evaluate the merits of their claim that Jesus was the Messiah.

But a number of religious leaders decided that a more stringent plan of action was necessary. The leader of this group was a young man named Saul. He was intelligent, dedicated, well-educated, and vicious. The text says he was "breathing out murderous threats against the Lord's disciples"[139] in the earliest days of the Church. He asked for permission from the high priest to visit the synagogues in the city of Damascus and round up any Jews who'd converted to Christianity, taking them as prisoners to Jerusalem. Permission was granted.

But something happened on the road to Damascus that changed things forever—both for Saul and for the early members of the Church. As he approached the city, a brilliant light shone down from the heavens and flashed around Saul and his companions. It was a terrifying experience, and Saul fell on the ground in fear.

Then he heard a voice call out from the light, "Saul, Saul, why do you persecute me?"[140] Dumbfounded, Saul asked who was speaking. "I am Jesus, whom you are persecuting," the voice answered. "Now get up and go into the city, and you will be told what you must do."[141]

When the light withdrew, Saul slowly got to his feet. He opened his eyes, intending to ask his companions if they'd just heard what he heard—but something was wrong. He could not see. He was blind. Even so, Saul knew that something incredible had just happened, and he made his way into the city of Damascus in obedience to God. But now he had a feeling it would be for a purpose far different from the one he originally intended.

A Fearless Firebrand

Days later, a Christian named Ananias received quite a shock when God spoke to him in a vision. "Go to the house of Judas on Straight Street and ask for a man from Tarsus named Saul, for he is praying," God said. "In a vision he [Paul] has seen a man named Ananias come and place his hands on him to restore his sight."[142]

Now, Ananias was no dummy. He knew Saul as a most zealous persecutor, and he knew what Saul planned to do with any Christians he found in Damascus. That being the case, Ananias was hesitant to make things worse for his fellow believers. But God was firm. He expected Ananias to trust Him, and know that all would work for their good.

So when Ananias found Saul, he made no effort to mince his words or hedge his bets: "Brother Saul," he said, "the Lord—Jesus, who appeared to you on the road as you were coming here—has sent me so that you may see again and be filled with the Holy Spirit."[143]

Immediately, "something like scales"[144] fell away from Saul's eyes, and he was able to see. And what he saw was a completely new world in which the truth appeared in a new light: Jesus was the Messiah revealed in the Scriptures, whom he'd been waiting for his entire life.

Without any delay, Saul was baptized as a member of this new Church. He became one of the very people he intended to throw in jail, and he didn't even give the matter a second thought. He'd been changed from the inside out.

As a former Pharisee, Saul was still young, persuasive, fearless, and well educated. But once he regained his strength, he began teaching in the synagogues of Damascus, telling everyone what had happened to him and boldly proclaiming the truth of Christ. His training in the Old Testament Scriptures allowed him to explain text after text, prophecy after prophecy, proving that Jesus was the Messiah and the key to salvation. He was very convincing and didn't care what dangerous opposition he might face.

At first the people were baffled. "Isn't he the man who raised havoc in Jerusalem among those who call on this name?" they asked. "And hasn't he come here to take them as prisoners to the chief priests?"[145] But Saul was steadfast in his preaching, and soon many people began to accept his words. People decided to follow Jesus. The Church grew.

There were still a number of religious leaders who wanted no part in listening to what the early Christians had to say—and they were especially vexed that someone like Saul had abandoned their ranks and defected to the group they saw as the enemy. So rather than continue to debate, they conspired to have him killed.

A Basket Case for Christ

Saul learned of their plans, however. With the help of certain Christians in Damascus—the very people he'd once sought to throw in prison—Saul was lowered over the city wall in a basket at night. The people who saw this merely thought that goods were being transported. After escaping, Saul traveled back to Jerusalem and met with Jesus's original disciples, learning more about what God was doing in their lives to help them become more like Christ. The Christian leaders, in turn, were amazed that God would take a fanatical enemy like Saul and turn him into an uncompromising proponent of their beliefs. And to this day we use the expression "Damascus road experience" to explain a major revelation that changes our thinking and behavior.

Key Bible Passage to Remember

"But the Lord said to Ananias, 'Go! This man is my chosen instrument to proclaim my name to the Gentiles and their kings and to the people of Israel.'" (Acts 9:15)

Saul later changed his name to Paul, and it was primarily through him that the Gospel spread out from Jerusalem and into many other parts of the world. Ironically, the man who'd persecuted believers in Jesus became a believer himself—and experienced much persecution for his newfound faith.

Begin and End It with a Bang

The End of the World
(Revelation 1:1–22:21)

As the main inhabitants of this planet, we're fascinated by what the end of it all will be like. We sure don't want it to happen during our lifetimes, yet we ponder the different causes and catalysts that might result in the destruction of a civilization like ours (which is how books like *The Road* and *The Hunger Games* come about).

Some theorize that the world began with a Big Bang. We wonder if the end will be devastating or, as the poet T. S. Eliot says, *"This is the way the world ends / Not with a bang but a whimper."* But a whimper would be anticlimactic, and the final book of the Bible says the world clearly ends with a bang.

It's no surprise, then, that many Bible readers have taken a special interest in its final book, Revelation. Written by John when he was the last surviving member of Jesus's original twelve apostles, this apocalyptic narrative provides a mysterious (and often confusing) window into the closing scenes of life on our planet. But John was only given symbols, not specific dates and times.

Both a Lion and a Lamb

John's vision starts with a vision of Jesus Christ, but not the kind of vision we're used to seeing in old framed pictures of a youngish, gentle Jesus, meek and mild. The now victorious Son of God is described not as a human being but as an all-powerful heavenly being: "The hair on his head was white like wool, as white as snow, and his eyes were like blazing fire. His feet were like bronze glowing in a furnace, and his voice was like the sound of rushing waters. In his right hand he held seven stars, and coming out of his mouth was a sharp, double-edged sword. His face was like the sun shining in all its brilliance."[146] Jesus was a descendant of the Jewish tribe of Judah, and in another place in the Bible is called the Lion of Judah. (You may recall the lion Aslan, a symbol of Jesus, in the Narnia movies.) All this is to say that the person in Revelation is someone whom the religious leaders who crucified Jesus wouldn't want to antagonize.

After receiving several messages for the Church communities in various regions throughout the world, encouraging them to hang in there even as they're being persecuted, John is pulled into a vision of God's throne room in heaven. He sees a wild and magnificent scene filled with thunder and lightning, thrones and crowns, a sea of glass, and strangely symbolic creatures singing songs of worship. The whole scene is a visual frenzy meant to communicate the awesome power and authority of God amid conflict with evil.

There's sadness in the throne room, too. Something has been broken, and at first no one can be found with the goodness and love and authority required to fix it. But then a sound of joy! The Lamb has come, "looking as if it had been slain"[147] (a reference to Him as the sacrificial Lamb on the cross), and He, Jesus, is worthy to lead the final battle. He is able to open the scroll that represents God's judgment on the sin and evil and pain present in the world throughout all time.

The judgment is terrible, but necessary in order to eradicate the sin and evil and pain that have plagued the world.

A Disaster Waiting to Happen

Shrouded in holiness, the Lamb begins breaking the seals that have held the scroll closed. The first four seals each unleash a terrible horse and rider upon the earth—what we often refer to as the four horsemen of the apocalypse. Those riders represent conquest, war, famine, and disease. These are terrible things, and yet we are meant to find comfort in the fact that all are under the authority of the Lamb. He alone has the power to bring them to an end.

When the Lamb breaks the fifth seal, the souls of the martyred cry out for justice. The Lamb hears them, but they are told to wait a little longer. Then the Lamb opens the sixth seal, and the world erupts in fiery chaos, during which the earth shakes, the sun turns black, and the moon becomes the color of blood. This is the day of God's wrath against all evil.

Before the seventh seal is broken, John's vision focuses on thousands upon thousands of men and women who are protected by God against the new disasters ready to strike the world. Then the Lamb breaks the seventh seal, producing seven trumpets, each declaring a new wave of judgment.

The first four trumpets bring various disasters. Hail and fire mixed with blood. A blazing mountain poisoning the sea. Stars falling from the sky. Light struck down from the heavens. The fifth trumpet opens an ancient abyss, filled with smoke and horrifying creatures. The sixth trumpet results in the death of a third of all the people still living on the earth. The seventh trumpet brings yet more destruction, more judgment—including seven bowls filled with plagues that ravage the earth.

John is shown even more. There is continued

rebellion against God, led by the personification of evil—Satan. There are dragons and beasts, fallen empires, and the Antichrist, a human with great power appearing to be the new Messiah, in place of Jesus. And yet the Lamb keeps all these disasters within bounds. He is sovereign over the destruction, and His judgment guides the cleansing and remaking of the world. Evil is defeated. God wins.

The Ultimate Happy Ending

The final chapters of Revelation include the more encouraging parts of John's vision. He is allowed to see a shadow of what things will look like when human beings take their place in God's heavenly kingdom—what the text calls "a new heaven and a new earth."[148] It's a wonderful thing to see.

Those who have accepted God's gift of salvation are introduced as "the bride, the wife of the Lamb."[149] They are loved and cherished by Jesus. Even better, God's people live with Him, just as Adam and Eve walked and talked with Him in the Garden of Eden—except in John's vision, the earthly garden is replaced by a heavenly city filled with brilliant light and unimaginable gifts from God.

This heavenly place is not reserved for a specific race or country. Rather, people from every tribe and language and nation gather around the throne and congregate together as members of God's kingdom.

The river of life flows down the center of the city, and the tree of life, initially forbidden to Adam and Eve, grows in abundance once more. Even more, "the leaves of the tree are for the healing of the nations."[150] All can now freely eat and grow into all God originally intended them to become.

In short, John's revelation makes it clear that the end of the world is not something to fear if you trust in Jesus's saving work on the cross. Because at its core, the end of this world, filled with suffering and pain, is really the beginning of something far, far better.

Key Bible Passage to Remember

"Look, I am coming soon! My reward is with me, and I will give to each person according to what they have done. I am the Alpha and the Omega, the First and the Last, the Beginning and the End." (Revelation 22:12–13)

The book of Revelation is tumultuous and sometimes perplexing. But it shows that Jesus is in charge of the first and last acts of the great drama, as well as everything in between, and that He will in the end make everything right. True justice and mercy will prevail, and nothing done on His behalf will go unrewarded.

About the Authors

James Stuart Bell is a Christian publishing veteran and the owner of Whitestone Communications, a literary development agency. He has received cover and inside credit for nearly 150 books.

Sam O'Neal is author of *Field Guide for Small Group Leaders* (InterVarsity Press) and a content editor for LifeWay Christian Resources. Read more from Sam at www.SamONealWrites.com.

Notes

1. Matthew 5:38
2. Job 19:20
3. Deuteronomy 32:10
4. Matthew 7:12
5. Matthew 5:44; 22:39
6. Exodus 20:1–17
7. Genesis 2:9
8. Genesis 2:9
9. Genesis 6:9
10. Genesis 6:20
11. Genesis 7:15
12. Genesis 7:11
13. Genesis 7:23
14. Genesis 9:7
15. Genesis 11:2
16. Genesis 11:4
17. Genesis 9:1
18. Genesis 3:5
19. Genesis 11:9
20. Genesis 11:10–26
21. Genesis 25:23
22. Genesis 25:27
23. Genesis 25:30

24. Genesis 25:31
25. Genesis 27:19
26. Genesis 37:4
27. Genesis 37:27
28. Genesis 39:4
29. Exodus 9:9
30. Judges 6:12
31. Judges 6:15
32. Judges 6:25–26
33. Judges 6:31
34. Judges 6:34
35. Judges 7:2
36. Judges 7:20
37. Judges 16:16
38. Judges 16:25
39. 1 Samuel 17:4
40. 1 Samuel 17:25
41. 1 Samuel 17:26
42. 1 Samuel 17:37
43. 1 Samuel 17:43
44. 1 Samuel 17:46
45. 1 Kings 18:19
46. 1 Kings 18:21
47. 1 Kings 18:24
48. 1 Kings 18:27
49. 1 Kings 18:27

50. 1 Kings 18:33
51. 1 Kings 18:36
52. 1 Kings 18:39
53. Daniel 6:3
54. Daniel 6:10
55. Daniel 6:20
56. Daniel 6:24
57. Esther 1:11
58. Esther 2:2
59. Esther 2:12
60. Esther 6:6
61. Esther 6:10
62. 2 Kings 14:25
63. Jonah 1:2
64. Jonah 1:3
65. Jonah 1:9
66. Jonah 1:12
67. Jonah 1:17
68. Jonah 2:10
69. Jonah 3:1
70. Jonah 3:4
71. Luke 1:30–31
72. Luke 1:34
73. Luke 1:35
74. Luke 2:10–11
75. John 2:3

76. John 2:4
77. John 2:8
78. Luke 15:13
79. Luke 15:16
80. Luke 15:18–19
81. Luke 15:20
82. Luke 15:29–30
83. Luke 10:25
84. Luke 10:29
85. Luke 10:30
86. Luke 10:35
87. Luke 10:36
88. Luke 10:37
89. Luke 10:37
90. Mark 6:47
91. Matthew 14:25
92. Matthew 14:27
93. Matthew 14:28
94. Matthew 14:29
95. Matthew 14:31
96. Mark 4:38–39
97. Luke 9:32
98. Matthew 17:2
99. Luke 9:29
100. Luke 9:33
101. Luke 9:35
102. Luke 9:38
103. Luke 9:43
104. Jennifer Valen-
    tino-DeVries,
    "Steve Jobs's Best
    Quotes," *The
    Wall Street Jour-
    nal*, August 24,
    2011.
105. See Luke 10:38–
    42, for example.
106. John 11:5
107. John 11:11
108. Luke 11:21
109. John 11:23
110. Luke 11:32
111. John 11:37
112. Luke 11:39
113. Luke 11:43
114. Matthew 26:18
115. Luke 22:19
116. Luke 22:20
117. John 13:8
118. John 13:27
119. Matthew 26:75
120. Luke 23:33
121. Luke 23:34
122. Matthew 27:40
123. Matthew 27:42
124. Luke 23:40-41
125. Luke 23:42
126. Luke 23:43
127. Matthew 27:46
128. John 19:30
129. Matthew 28:3
130. Matthew 28:4
131. Matthew 28:8
132. Luke 24:16
133. Luke 24:49
134. Acts 2:3
135. Acts 2:7–8
136. Joel 2:28–32
137. Acts 2:23
138. Acts 2:37
139. Acts 9:1
140. Acts 9:4
141. Acts 9:5-6
142. Acts 9:11–12
143. Acts 9:17
144. Acts 9:18
145. Acts 9:21
146. Revelation
    1:14–16
147. Revelation 5:6
148. Revelation 21:1
149. Revelation 21:9
150. Revelation 22:2

Index